# Bush Teacher In B.C.

# Bush Teacher In B.C.

Dr. June Temple

WELCH PUBLISHING COMPANY INC.
Burlington, Ontario, Canada

First Printing 1985
Second Printing 1987

ISBN: 1-55011-001-2

Welch Publishing Company Inc.
960 The Gateway
Burlington, Ontario
L7L 5K7   Canada

Printed in Canada

# TABLE OF CONTENTS

CHAPTER I          East to West                         1

CHAPTER II         Forty Years of Preparation           9

CHAPTER III        Plenty of Work                      14

CHAPTER IV         Training for Service                21

CHAPTER V          Sabbatical from Teaching            39

CHAPTER VI         Classes Begun                       56

CHAPTER VII        A Full Dorm                         96

CHAPTER VIII       Another Move                       122

CHAPTER IX         Gospel Team Trips                  143

CHAPTER X          A Job Finished                     169

BIBLIOGRAPHY                                          188

## ACKNOWLEDGEMENT

To my daughter Pauline for her long hours spent in correcting, spelling, editing and typing the manuscript for this book.

# PURPOSE

This autobiography has been written to share the joys and sorrows, the comical times, the trying times and the spiritual battles that one missionary and her family experienced. It has been written to show the humanness of one person who was chosen by the Lord to serve Him in a special way.

Another purpose for which it was written was to give some insight into native life, culture, beliefs, and thinking in order to better understand some of the battles that a missionary family faces when working with these people.

Lastly, it was written to put a burden in Christian hearts to reach the lost Indians, Eskimos and Aluets of North America for Christ.

Written for the glory of God and dedicated to my husband, Chuck, and our four children, Pauline, Patti, Charles and David. Through their help, prayers, and support, my years on the mission field were blessed.

# Chapter I

The evening before Charle's and David's school closed for Christmas the thermometer read minus thirty-five degrees. Chuck went out to try to start the travel-all and wonder of wonders, the engine turned over with no problem. Since we were planning on going south for Christmas, Chuck thought we had better pack and leave because colder weather was predicted and he didn't know if we would ever get the car started in the morning. What followed was a never to be forgotten trip. It took twenty-four hours to travel five hundred miles.

First of all, the heater was not working; so everyone except the driver (we each took turns driving) sat in sleeping bags in the car. We drove thirty-five miles and stopped at a gas station to see if the heater could be fixed. There was no one in the station to fix heaters at ten o'clock at night. We drove seventy five miles further and stopped at another gas station with a repeat performance; no one to fix the heater.

Fifty miles more were travelled and we stopped for gas and hot chocolate. Then the car wouldn't start and two hours were spent by garage attendants trying to get the engine going. When it started, we drove for two more hours and stopped at another station. It was now my turn to drive and I drove out of the station, proceeded one block and the engine died. Since we were on a hill and there was a gas station at the bottom of the hill, I coasted down into this station, where we spent three hours trying to get the car started. Part of that time, I slept sitting on the counter by the sink in the ladies washroom, because, it was the only place I could find warm and I felt like an icycle. Whenever a lady came into the washroom I would wake enough to see the startled expression on her face over finding someone sitting practically in the sink. The reason I chose this perch was because it was the only spot that the heat from the ceiling vent reached.

It was now morning and we were starved. Neither Chuck nor I had any money left. Charles said David had some Christmas money with him. So, we woke David, who was sound asleep in the back of the travel-all in his sleeping bag, and he gladly shared his money for breakfast.

The temperature still was remaining way below zero and a wind had come up which made it feel twice as cold. I drove out of the gas station and about a mile out of town a tire went flat. Rather than risk the engine cutting out, the tire was changed with the car in neutral and my foot accelerating the gas pedal when needed.

The next six hours went smoothly and again it was my turn to drive.

The travel-all had a tendency to jump backward when passing through the reverse gear into drive. This happened when we were ready to leave the border and the official was passing in back of our car. Fortunately, he was not touched physically, but he was mentally and vocally unhappy.

About five miles south of the border, freezing rain had been falling for several hours. We ended partially in a ditch and had to wait until someone with a heavy enough vehicle came along to pull us out.

How exhausted we were and how good it felt to finally reach Seattle.

Now, let's go back and begin the main story in Pennsylvania in the year nineteen sixty-seven, three years before the missionary service began. I was teaching music at a Christian school; Chuck, my husband, was a supervisor for the Boeing Aircraft Corporation; and our four children, (Pauline, Patti, Charles and David), attended school.

In the Spring of nineteen sixty-seven, Boeing decided to transfer Chuck to the Seattle, Washington plant and moved him and the furniture west. Naturally, the rest of us went along and we settled into a new home, new jobs and new schools. Then the time was spent seeking a new church home. For one year, churches were visited and evaluated. Finally, one was found that passed all qualifications. The Word was preached and the Love of God could be felt among the people in the congregation.

Shortly after my family became involved in many aspects of this church's life, a mission director spoke at the church. Rev. John Gillespie presented his mission's ministry in the Arctic among native people. One arm of the ministry was a high school in Alaska. In the planning stages, was a similar ministry in British Columbia. As the director explained in detail the need for teachers, I began to feel that this was where the Lord wanted me to teach.

On the way home from church that night, I asked Chuck what he thought of the speaker's message and the answer was, 'Oh, it was all right'. I felt strongly that the Lord wanted us on this mission field and yet I did not want to influence my husband on such an important matter. I wondered how I should pray about the matter and the idea came to pray, 'Lord, if you want us on the mission field make my husband dissatisfied at work'. This would be a sign to me confirming the Lord's will and the prayer became a daily one.

Chuck had a comfortable position at Boeing. His hours were convenient and the salary sufficient for daily needs and some pleasures. In a few months though a portion of scripture that appears several times in the New Testament 'the labourer is worthy of his reward' began to repeat itself in Chuck's mind. He had very little peace because he felt that his salary was too high for the amount of work required. So, he went to his supervisor and told the man that he felt he could handle some more work.

In a few more months, Boeing began to experience financial difficulties due to contract losses. Employees began to be laid off or else had to take a reduction in job position or salary or both.

By the fall of nineteen sixty-nine, Chuck was working twelve hours a day, seven days a week. He had been transferred to another plant which added another hour's drive going to and coming from work. This totalled fourteen hours from the time he left home at four a.m. until he returned home at night. His pay was cut quite a bit. He had also been reduced several levels in job position. Physically, Chuck was exhausted by the long hours. Emotionally, Chuck missed his family life and the pressure of financial problems had begun to pinch. Spiritually, Chuck was starved with little time for devotional or church life.

Finally, the Boeing doctor advised Chuck to take a few days off. During this time Chuck discussed with me what the Lord was trying to tell us. It was at this time, that I told Chuck how I had been praying and Chuck's response was, 'Well, we better find out where the Lord wants us'.

When the Christmas holiday came, I spent some time sending out letters to different areas of Christian service (one of which was Arctic Missions) asking for job applications. Chuck and I had discussed full time service with all four children and each of them felt that if the Lord wanted us as a family on the mission field that was where they wanted to be.

Job applications quickly came in the mail and were filled out. Each family member started to pray that the Lord would close doors so that the only place of service, where the Lord wanted us to be, would be the open door. Chuck and I also prayed that the open door would be a place where both of our abilities could be used and not just one of ours.

In January of nineteen seventy a missionary from Arctic Missions stopped at the church. Chuck and I were sponsors of the 'college and career' young peoples group at church and we asked the missionary, Gene Parkins, to speak at the evening meeting.

Gene told how two missionary families had moved down into British Columbia from Alaska. Two new families had come with the mission and they were all settled into an area known as Chilanko Forks and were working with the Chilcotin Indians. He told of the search for property to build a school. Then Gene ended by telling about the need for young peoples' groups to come help the missionaries for a week or two.

The College and Career group was impressed and began to discuss the possibility of going up to British Columbia to help during spring break at college. The decision was made to go, providing all financial and other details could be worked out.

Spring break was in March in nineteen seventy and this gave the young people two months to make known to the church the British Columbia missionaries' needs and the college and career group's decision to go help. There was transportation to be arranged, food to be planned, finances for gas and food to be raised and the need for another adult to be willing to give of his time to go.

Chuck didn't think that he would be able to get time off and thought he could not go. But, when he asked his boss for time off the boss said, 'Sure, go ahead'.

The Sunday night in March before it was time to leave for British Columbia it seemed that all arrangements for the trip had been taken care of except, financially the group was a hundred dollars short. The young people were all in the back of the church feeling despondent because it seemed that they would not be able to make the trip, due to lack of funds. Then our daughter Pauline, a member of the college and career group, came running up with a check in her hand that a man in the church had given her. The check was for a hundred dollars made out to the church.

Chuck said, 'Pauline, you better go back to that man and make sure the check is for our use'. When it was confirmed that the check was for the young people's use, despondency turned to joy.

The following Saturday morning, early, three vehicles with three adults, twenty-six young people, food for a week, suitcases and sleeping bags headed north.

Our plan had been to camp overnight since the drive from Seattle to Chilanko Forks, British Columbia would take about sixteen hours. But as the caravan pushed north they noticed that the campgrounds were closed and covered with snow. The drive itself was awe inspiring, winding through the beautiful Fraser Canyon. We were on a two lane paved road with sheer cliffs on one side and a deep gorge on the other. At the bottom of the gorge flowed the swift, mighty Fraser River.

Upon arriving in the town of Williams Lake, British Columbia around five p.m. a call was made to the pastor of the Baptist Church to ask permission to camp in the church's basement. Permission was granted and everyone began settling in.

Oven fried chicken was on the menu for supper that night. I turned the church oven on, put the chicken in and in about fifteen minutes the entire basement of the church was filled with smoke. The bottom of the oven had been grease spattered from some previous meal. So, doors and windows were opened and the chicken continued to cook. When the meal was served, several of the young people declared that 'that was the best smoked chicken they had ever eaten'.

After dinner dishes had been cleaned, some games played, a sing song and devotions, the tired group turned in. The girls and I unrolled our sleeping bags on one Sunday School room floor; Chuck, the other counsellor and the fellows on another Sunday School room floor for a good but short sleep.

Everyone was up before the crack of dawn for the last and somewhat dangerous part of the trip. A hundred and twelve miles of narrow, rutty, deep and steep, gravel road which took four hours to travel. The scenery was beautiful along the way but everyone was happy to finally arrive at their destination.

Chilanko Forks turned out to be a small logging community nestled in a great forest. A small lumber mill was at one edge of the village. Here white people from the village and Indians from a nearby reserve worked. There was an abandoned Canadian Forces base at the other side of the village. Still existing was a landing strip and a few of the buildings which were being used for a weather station. The mission had bought eight homes from the air base personnel who had been transferred. Around the area, outside of Chilanko Forks, were cattle ranches and also resorts (on beautiful lakes) famous for summer fishing and fall hunting.

Chuck and I, plus the young women stayed in one of the homes. This house had inside washing facilities, wood heating and a big old wood stove for me to cook the meals on. Electricity was had for a few hours in the morning and evening, produced by a light-plant.

Besides Pauline being a part of the group, Patti also was a member and home from college for the spring break. So, both girls were in the house with Chuck and myself.

John Patterson, the third counsellor, and all the fellows were in a cabin which had no modern facilities. The little house out back was to some a curiosity since they had never before used an outhouse. It was also a great place for pranksters to lock someone in. When this happened yells and shouts could be heard all over the village.

Five of the fellows who were in this cabin were from the church's high school youth group. Our two sons, Charles and David, were two of the five.

By March of nineteen seventy the snow had disappeared from the Chilanko Forks area. But the air was cold and from time to time a few flakes could be seen falling. At night all the Seattle people wore their heavy jackets, but, still they shivered with the temperatures dropping below freezing. Each afternoon was comfortable with the sun usually shining brightly.

Five days went very quickly with so much to do. Some of the fellows were put to work breaking open a frozen well and putting in a new casement. The rest of the fellows were assigned to wood detail. This consisted of going out and cutting down dead trees, limbing them and going through the whole process necessary to bring in firewood for the four missionary families who lived at Chilanko Forks. For an average winter each family used ten cords of wood since they used it as their only source of heat.

Girls who typed helped get out thank you letters and anything else that needed typing. Other girls cut out flannelgraph materials for the women missionaries to use in their children's services. When these two jobs were finished all the girls helped with spring house cleaning in different homes.

Each evening the missionaries and the youth group met together for a time of singing, testimonies and devotions. Many of the young people yielded themselves completely to the Lord during this time. Some later went into full time service.

One young man came up to Chuck after the evening get-together and said, 'I want you to cut my shoulder length hair right now. I let it grow in rebellion to my father and want to get rid of it'. Scissors were borrowed and the cutting began by electricity, but, the lights went out when his head was half cut; so the job was fininshed by flashlight.

The next day one of the leaders of the wood cutting

detail, Stoney Nicklie, an Indian, asked 'Whatever happened to that guy with the long hair?' The newly shorn young man answered, 'He's gone forever'. Stoney had a good laugh when he learned what had happened.

On the last afternoon that the group could remain at Chilanko Forks, the missionaries took all the young people and their counsellors out to a lake for a hot dog roast and picnic. Games were played and all the Seattle people experienced something new, which was WALKING ON WATER. That is, frozen water, eighteen inches thick.

An exciting, memorable time was over and the drive home was long since there was no time for an overnight stop.

# Chapter II

All of Chuck's life, he had thought that a missionary was one who went around with a Bible under his arm and did nothing but evangelize and teach. While he was up at Chilanko Forks, Chuck saw the need for all kinds of back-up ministries on the mission field and felt, for the first time, that the Lord could use him there.

In the year nineteen twenty-one, Chuck was born, the youngest of six children, into a Christian home. The family's whole life revolved around church meetings and activities. In their church each Sunday there were two morning meetings, Sunday School in the afternoon, then two meetings in the evening. The entire day was spent either in church or walking to and from the church. Then, in the summertime Daily Vacation Bible School was held for the whole month of July.

As a very small boy, Chuck learned the Scriptures at his mother's knee. Many a time he would want to go out to play and his mother's response was, 'after you learn one more verse'. Chuck accepted the Lord as a child. Later in life, when temptations came, the Holy Spirit would bring one or more of the memorized verses to mind. Sometimes Chuck would ignore the Spirit's wooing but other times he would be able to withstand the temptation. But, never in his life did he feel that the mission field was for him. Following the trip north he thought differently about his usefulness on the mission field.

A short time after returning home from Chilanko Forks, Chuck's mind started to fill with thoughts of job security, pension benefits, three weeks paid vacations and ideas of Christian service were put in the back recesses of his mind. In the next few months the Lord had two more lessons for Chuck to learn.

Early in April, Chuck did not have to work one Sunday and part of the message he heard at the morning service was on James, chapter one, verse eight. 'A double minded man is unstable in all his ways'. To Chuck it seemed that the Lord was speaking right to him. When he was serving the Lord at Chilanko Forks that was where he wanted to be. When he was working at Boeing, that seemed best financially. During the following weeks, this message came repeatedly to his thoughts.

The first week of May was Chuck's turn to drive the car pool to work. He left home at four a.m. to pick up his five passengers. It was a rainy, especially dark morning. After they had been on the road about forty-five minutes a terrible accident loomed in the headlights on the freeway ahead of them. Several cars had collided, exploded and were furiously burning. There was no room to stop and by a miracle the Temple's car passed through the middle of two burning piles of cars unscathed.

All the men in the car were shouting and praising Chuck for his excellent driving, but, Chuck said it was the Lord's hand on the wheel and not his own that got them through the terrible accident. Chuck knew his life had been preserved that day for a reason.

Satanic forces were trying to discourage Chuck from going into full time service, but, the Lord was the Victor in each of the battles.

In the meantime, I was under attack also. A fear of danger for my children's safety kept coming to my mind. Fear that they would be injured or even their lives taken if they went to the mission field.

One week Charles' high school secretary called for me to come get him. He had had a concussion during gym time. Another week David came home from school with a dislocated shoulder from wrestling club. Each time the Lord undertook in that a possibly serious injury was quickly healed.

At night, I would often wake with a sense of a Satanic presence in the bedroom. I would call upon the name of the Lord and immediately the presence would leave. Then, I would be able to return to peaceful sleep.

During my break time at Seattle Christian School, I would often find an empty classroom to sit and play the piano for relaxation. The school had purchased a new hymnal and I was enjoying going through it playing old and new songs. Newer hymns were always fun to play and either read to myself or sing softly the words. It seemed like each time I did this now I kept returning to one song in particular. A song I had heard before but never really studied. Now the words had a special meaning for me and I could not help the tears rolling down my face with each verse.

So send I you to labour unrewarded,
To serve unpaid, unloved, unsought, unknown
To bear rebuke, to suffer scorn and scoffing
So send I you to toil for Me, alone.

So send I you to bind the bruised and broken,
O'er wand'ring souls to work, to weep, to wake,
To bear the burdens of a world a-weary
So send I you to suffer for My sake.

So send I you to loneliness and longing,
With heart a hung'ring for the loved and known,
Forsaking home and kindred, friend and dear one
So send I you to know My love alone.

So send I you to leave your life's ambition,
To die to dear desire, self-will resign,
To labour long and love where men revile you
So send I you to lose your life in Mine.

So send I you to hearts made hard by hatred,
To eyes made blind because they will not see,
To spend-tho it be blood · to spend and spare not
So send I you to taste of Calvary.

'As the Father hath sent Me,
So send I you'[1]

Following this hymn one other always seemed to be
needed to be played. Again the tears flowed, but not for
myself this time. Instead, they flowed because of the ex-
ceeding great love of my Lord and what this love cost
Him.

He Was Wounded For Our Transgressions

He was wounded for our transgressions,
He bore our sins in His body on the tree;
For our guilt He gave us peace,
From our bondage gave release,
And with His stripes, and with His stripes
And with His stripes our souls are healed.

---

1. Compiled by John W. Peterson, Singing Youth,
Zondervan Publishing House (Grand Rapids, 1966) p. 219

He was numbered among transgressors,
We did esteem Him forsaken by His God,
As our sacrifice He died,
That the law be satisfied,
And all our sin, and all our sin,
And all our sin was laid on Him.

We had wandered, we all had wandered
Far from the fold of 'the Shepherd of the sheep';
But he sought us where we were,
On the mountains bleak and bare,
And brought us home, and brought us home,
And brought us safely home to God.

Who can number His generations?
Who shall declare all the triumphs of His cross?
Millions, dead, now live again,
Myriads follow in his train!
Victorious Lord, victorious Lord,
Victorious Lord and coming King![2]

By the middle of May, answers from all application forms had been received and there was only one door open; that of Arctic Missions. A couple of places only needed Chuck or me, not both. Others didn't have any openings, but Arctic Missions needed dorm parents at the school that they were opening in British Columbia.

As the mission considered our four teenage children who knew and loved the Lord, they felt that Chuck and I had been given a gift in the counselling and training of young people. The position of dorm parents was one the mission wanted us to assume.

We as a family now knew where the Lord wanted us to serve. So, after nineteen years and eleven months of work at Boeing, Chuck gave his two weeks' notice and on the first day of June was no longer employed. Pauline had finished her third year of college and Patti her first. The two boys, finishing grades ten and nine, were ready for summer recess. I gave notice to the Christian school that at the end of the semester, I was no longer available for teaching.

The second week of June we all travelled back east to tell family and friends what the Lord had called us to do.

---

2. Peterson, Op. Cit., p. 64.

Then we returned to Seattle to pack and put our furniture into storage before heading north the middle of July.

It seemed that the Lord's cleansing and purifying for service was just about complete. On the last Sunday before going to British Columbia, I was asked to sing during the morning service.

After praying and seeking the Lord's guidance, I felt the Lord's leading to choose the sacred song 'The Stranger of Galilee'. While practicing at home, I would question myself as to whether I would become emotional when singing but absolutely saw no reason for this to happen. There was perfect peace and calm as I sang but during the last verse, when I got to the words, 'He bids me go and the story tell' the tears started to fall. Not only on my face but also on almost every face in the congregation.

When I sat down my oldest son whispered 'Mother, that was terrible' but I knew it was the Lord's doing. My family was prepared to go to the field and the church was prepared to back us in prayer.

## Chapter III

A very crowded car travelled north from Seattle to visit the mission compound for the summer. Besides the six of us, there was a dog, two cats, a trunk full of suitcases and a car top carrier full of boxes. The car rode very low to the ground and didn't travel very speedily.

Our destination was one hundred miles northwest of Williams Lake, where we had had the delicious 'smoked chicken' the previous March. Travel through the beautiful Fraser Canyon was just as awe inspiring as before. The road was paved and good up to the town of Quesnel and six miles past when it turned into a very narrow, windy, up hill and down dale gravel road. There was room for two cars to pass each other in some spots and not in others. Logging trucks also traveled this road and usually the spot where a car met a logging truck was the extra narrow one.

Property for the Canadian school, which was named 'The Native Institute of Canada' had been purchased in April. It consisted of a hundred and sixty acres on which was an old two room cabin, a shed, a barn and a soddie. The meadow and buildings were surrounded by tall Jack Pine and Aspen trees.

During the month of June some men had come up from the States to cut trees and peel logs for the construction of three buildings. When we arrived in mid-July, all three foundations were set and one building had the log side walls up. The next building had part of the log walls up and the third building was just a foundation.

Gene Parkins (the missionary who spoke to our college and career group), his wife Helen and their three small children were living in a camper between the old cabin and the first building under construction. Gene was supervising the summer building program and was to be the director of the Native Institute of Canada.

The old cabin on the property had cots in one room, where young men who were helping slept. The barn also had young men sleeping in the hay.

One family helping with construction during July, was

living in a tent. Another family, who was there to help, was living in a one room hunter's cabin on a beautiful lake about a half mile from the school site.

Pauline, Patti, Chuck and I rented another hunter's cabin at the lake while Charles and David opted to sleep in the barn. The rent for the cabin for a month was thirty dollars. There was no electricity or running water but the room did have two double beds and a wood stove.

Everyone ate their meals together in the two room cabin on the Native Institute of Canada property. The room had a wood cook stove and a large kitchen table and chairs. On one end of the room were cabinets and work space. All the women worked together in preparing the food. Usually breakfast was eaten inside because the air was very cold. By noon the sun had warmed the temperature outside and the wood cook stove heated the cabin inside to an unbearable temperature so that everyone decided to eat at picnic tables outside.

One of the ladies brought with her from the states sour dough starter. Many a morning she prepared sour dough pancakes which were her specialty and yummy. She also fixed sour dough biscuits and bread all of which the hard working men and women ate in large quantities.

This lady and her husband who came to help were also seeking the Lord's leading for service. They later came with the mission to serve in Alaska.

Another couple, young, newly married, came in a camper for a week to help and observe. They too, later became part of Arctic Missions staff.

When July ended, we as a family moved into the two room cabin on the Native Institute of Canada property. Chuck and I put our sleeping bags on two cots in the room where the table and cook stove stood. The other room was built like the leg of an L to the first room. Pauline and Patti had cots in one end of the L and Charles and David had theirs at the other end. During the day, the two empty cots of Chuck's and mine fit perfectly in the open space of the L to give more space around the table in the kitchen.

This cabin was made of logs with moss chinked in between the logs to keep out any drafts. The cabin's most unique feature was a floor that slanted. In the kitchen, the table slanted and Chuck sat at the low end. Everytime anything was spilled it ended in Chuck's lap.

Young people and families from our home church in Seattle came up to visit and to help during the summer.

Some had campers to sleep in while others were squeezed into the cabin or else the barn.

People from other churches, who had an interest in this new school, would also come to help. It was interesting that when a specific trade was needed, for example, a plumber, or an electrician, etc. a car would come up the driveway to the Native Institute of Canada and the driver would ask, 'Do you need a plumber, electrician, etc?' Yes, would be the answer and it would be explained to him that he was a direct answer to prayer.

Most people chipped in toward the cost of groceries. Either with food they had brought with them or else cash. There were times though, as I prepared to go in to town to buy the groceries, that I knew I did not have enough money to buy all that was needed.

Before I reached the car someone would come to me and give me some money to cover part of the cost of the food. Always it was enough to cover the needed amount to buy all the groceries.

Everyone who came always remarked on the beauty of the area. Beyond the trees that surrounded the property, were green rolling hills. Every day the sky was an exquisite blue with puffy white clouds as the summer of nineteen seventy was a very dry one for the Cariboo country. The rustic buildings made the whole scene even more picturesque.

Many, as they were relaxing on the old cabin's porch; or sitting on the fence that surrounded the property; or laying on the bank of the creek that flowed by the barn; would say something about the great peace that they felt. They experienced the presence of God in a way that they never could at home with the noise, pressure and congestion of most urban and some rural areas.

There was no phone. The light plant was not used because daylight that far north was from four a.m. to eleven p.m. during the summer months. Therefore, no light plant noise. No traffic sounds crowded in and the silence struck most people. All this played a part in allowing the Holy Spirit to speak to people involved in the summer ministry of helps.

Days were long with the men trying to get as much accomplished as possible for the buildings to be ready for September use. For the ladies, the length of the day's chores were twice what they were used to because of no modern conveniences.

Helen Parkins, Pauline, Patti and I were up early to get the wood cooking stove heated enough to cook and serve breakfast for up to twenty people. No dishwasher was available, not even hot water was available.

A hundred and twenty feet from the cabin was a well which had a pump. The water was pumped into a milk can, hauled to the cabin (by one of the men) then dipped into a kettle or pan and heated on the stove for dishes (or personal washing). The dishes were then washed and rinsed in dish pans and towel dried.

A kerosene refrigerator in the old cabin was a great help for keeping food cold. Clothes washing was done out in the yard with an old wringer washer. The light plant was turned on long enough to do the wash, but the water for washing clothes was hauled from the creek and not heated. Even in August the water was frigid on hands but surprisingly the clothes came clean with the use of 'Arctic Power' cold water soap. Clothes were then hung on a line to dry in the sun and clean air. How sweet they smelled!

During all this work, I kept thinking 'What are you doing here' or else 'Look at all this work and you could have had a life of ease'. Satan was working double time whispering these ideas into my ears to cause discouragement.

I was born into the home of Lulu Blanche and James Edward Speake in the year of nineteen hundred and twenty-six. My sister Ruth and brother George were fourteen and eleven years older. I was a greatly loved little one with the kind of love that is only possible in a Christian home. The Speake families lives revolved around church and family ties.

Dad Speake was a Postal Inspector and away from home much. Discipline and home care was mother's responsibility, and although she was a very gentle person, she believed in 'tough love' in rearing her children.

When I was five years of age, my family moved to another section of Philadelphia. The home was larger and the family acquired help to do the cleaning. Laundry was sent out and chores for the children were nil.

Part of the work of a Postal Inspector was apprehending criminals. Jim Speake and his family had been threatened by several criminals whom he had captured and who had been sent to jail. I was carefully protected and watched.

There were no children close to my home and I was

not allowed to go any distance looking for playmates because of the danger my parents feared.

What filled my time with no chores and no playmates? My mother played games with me, read to me, rocked me and sang to me; played the piano while I sat at her side and taught me all types of handiwork. When I reached eight, I expressed a desire to learn to play the piano and a teacher was found to come to the home to give me lessons. My big joy, when I got home from school was to practice the piano for hours. After three years of study, it became necessary for me to stop the lessons but pleasure for playing the piano never ceased.

At twelve, I was singing with everyone on the radio, whether a popular singer or an opera singer. So, my parents decided that it was time for voice lessons. Again, there was plenty of time to practice and I enjoyed the daily time of vocalizing and practicing. (My voice lessons continued for nine years)

By mid-teens, my aspiration was to become a concert singer or else sing in Broadway Musicals or else become a part of the then famous Fred Waring Chorale. I was training toward this end when I accepted the Lord as my Saviour. I knew from that time on that I could never sing for the world but only for the Lord.

During the last few years in high school, I was taking the music course, singing in the concert choir and also the church choir. I continued voice lessons, gave concerts and was soloist for church programs but I decided that I would like to become a missionary nurse.

The second world war was on and following high school graduation, I applied to the Cadet Nurse Corps of the service. I thought that this would be a good place to get my training but was turned down by the Corps because I did not have enough science courses in high school due to being in the music course.

Apparently the door to nursing was shut, but I thought I would tackle it from another angle. First, I would go to a Christian college and then later into nurses' training. I applied to 'The King's College' and was accepted as a fall student.

I had three great roommates whose names also began with J. We were known as the four J's; Jane, Joanne, Janet and June. The teachers were excellent but the subjects seemed very difficult to me. In January, I became sick due to the pressure and worry about making good grades. I had to stay at home in bed for a month and there realized that the Lord did not design me to be a nurse. I also thought that the door to the mission field was closed for me.

When I returned for spring quarter, I changed my major to that of music and never had any more problems with subjects or grades in college.

During my sophomore year the second world war ended and one of the returning soldiers was Chuck, whom I met for the first time, at a Sunday evening young peoples' meeting at my church. It was attraction at first glance and Chuck pursued his interest with no hesitation. We had a good time together either in a group with family or friends or else just together on a date.

Musically by this time, I had sung in many recitals and concerts. I was the soloist for the college choir and had sung in many large churches, music halls, and convention centers in the Delaware and Pennsylvania area. In the spring, I received an invitation in the mail from an Opera company inviting me to come audition for soprano parts in the coming season's opera schedule. This did not interest me because I knew it was not God's plan for my life.

The main event of my junior year was an engagement ring. Then four months after college graduation Chuck and I were married. For the next fifteen years, my days were filled with being a wife and mother. They were busy and very happy times. A few other interests filled my spare time. A couple of afternoons a week and on Saturday morning young people came to my home for piano lessons. I was junior choir director, church soloist, Sunday School teacher, pianist and active in the Women's Missionary society.

Both my husband and I were involved with our children's activities (Scouts, sports, school and church events). All of us enjoyed camping together. Each summer our vacation was planned around a trip with our little tent trailer.

The Lord began to impress me with the future cost of college education for the children. To fulfill the desire to help with this cost would require a teaching certificate for the state of Pennsylvania. So, I went to Temple University to acquire the certificate and a second degree. Then, when my youngest child was in the fourth grade, I began to teach music in the public school. The hours were perfect for someone with a family because they were the same as the children's. I was in school when they were there and home when they were.

After two years of teaching in the public school, the hassle of discipline began to be very offensive to me and I changed positions to a Christian school.

All of this, unbeknown to me, was preparation by the Lord for a future missionary life; a prospect that I had thought no longer possible since college days.

# Chapter IV

At the Native Institute of Canada, halfway through August, the first building was completed enough for the Parkin's family to move in. Oh, there was still plenty of finishing to do, but the interior walls were up and the plumbing was connected. They could even take a bath because an electric pump had been obtained and when the light plant was running, water could run also. Gladly, Gene, Helen, Nancy, Vicki and John-John moved from the camper to the house.

All summer long Chuck, the children and I had been taking a bar of soap to the nearest lake for a bath. There was a spot where Tibbles Lake ran into Baker Creek (which ran through the Native Institute of Canada property) that was just like a bath tub. It was perfect to sit in with the lake water splashing over our shoulders then washing on down into the creek. This water was pleasantly warmed by the sun since the lake was shallow for quite a distance before entering the creek. But nights were getting below freezing this late in the summer and the water was getting too cold for lake baths. So, the old familiar round tub placed in the warm kitchen became our bath tub at the old cabin. Of course, Chuck and the boys had to sit outside or in the bedroom when we ladies bathed and visa versa.

In building the log homes at the Native Institute of Canada, instead of notching the logs at the corners, Hudson Bay corners were used. Two, two by ten boards were set on end at right angles, then each log was pinned by long spikes through the board. Eventually, a log was to be raised vertically between the two by ten's to give a finished appearance.

As the outside walls were raised, holes were drilled vertically through three logs for the placement of rebar to reinforce the walls. This procedure was followed through every three logs placed.

Charles and David were having a great summer learning the art of building log homes and assisting the men. One afternoon as the rebar was being hammered into the logs, it hit a knot and flew back out hitting Charles in the eye. By the time Charles had walked to the old cabin, his eye was completely filled internally with blood and bright red in color. He could not see in the one eye.

As I drove Charles the thirty-three miles into town for medical help what usually took an hour to drive was accomplished in forty-five minutes. We skidded around many narrow corners, the gravel flew and fortunately we met no logging trucks. Just as we reached the edge of town, Charles sat up in the back seat and said 'I can see'. I took him on into the doctors, who examined the eye and said that it was just badly bruised. Everyone back at the mission had been praying and our merciful Lord touched Charles' eye. In a few days the bloody appearance disappeared and no eye trouble resulted from the injury.

In looking at the work completed this last month of the summer, it became apparent that the buildings would not be ready for a fall school opening. Just a few students had applied for school the fall of nineteen seventy and they were notified that school would not open until the fall of nineteen seventy-one.

The mission decided that since Chuck and I were not needed immediately as dorm parents it would be wise for us to attend Boot Camp. This was a fourteen week course for new mission personnel and held out at Chilanko Forks (where we had previously taken the youth group). The course started right after Labour Day and finished the end of the first week in December.

Chuck and I decided not to take Charles and David with us to Chilanko Forks because there was no high school there. The Parkins' had graciously offered to care for our boys and they could take the bus, with the Parkins' two grade school girls, into Quesnel. The bus first stopped at the grade school and then went on to the high school. Everyone agreed that this would be good for the short three months that we had to be away.

But, before Chuck and I were to leave for Chilanko Forks we had a very important appointment to keep in the city of Prince George with immigration. We had applied for landed immigrant status, which was necessary to permanently reside and work in Canada. All the paperwork had been completed and the two of us went to Prince George for our interview.

The meeting with the immigration official turned out to be very interesting. We learned that Chuck would be graded and a certain number of points were needed to gain immigrant status. The wife was not considered at all.

First, points were determined by age. If under thirty-five, ten points were given. For every year over thirty-five, a point was taken away. Since Chuck was in his late forties he had no points for age.

The next determining factor was education. For every so many years of education one point was given. Chuck had thirteen points now.

Immigration's last factor was job classification, which was determined by the association between the job held in the states and that which was to be held in Canada. There was no association between Boeing supervisor and Missionary. The official had a huge job classification book and even though he tried he could not find any way to give points in this area.

The official apologized and said that Chuck was not eligible for landed immigrant status. He advised us that we could appeal the decision through Ottawa and that we should reapply from the states and not while visiting in Canada. Then, he said that Chuck had twenty-four hours to get out of the country and gave him a paper to hand in at the border when he left.

Since I did not have to leave the country, Chuck and Charles drove down to the border and handed the paper in. While in the states, the new application was mailed to Ottawa and the next day, Chuck and Charles again passed through the border. This time Chuck handed in another legal paper from the Canadian government that had been issued to us giving us permission to attend the training at Chilanko Forks.

When Labor Day arrived the two buildings beside the Parkins' house had the log walls in place and roofs on ready to stand a Cariboo winter. Building had gone smoothly that summer, except for one incident. When the roof joists of the last building were all in place, one of them tipped and they all went over like dominoes. Some of the joists needed repairs, then all were replaced and the roof finished.

The summer was over, Pauline and Patti had returned to the states to their respective schools. Our two boys were settled into a room at the Parkins' home. So, in beautiful sunshine, through beautiful fall colors, and picturesque scenery, Chuck and I rattled over to Chilanko Forks in a big old International Travel-all that had been given to us in August.

Chuck and I were given another two room home to live in at Chilanko Forks. It was located on the top of a hill and one room had a large window to view the homes below, the Lumber Mill and a small creek all settled in the lovely yellow Aspen and green Pine trees.

This room had a wood cook stove and a small round wood heating stove, a table and two chairs. One wall had a sink in it with a drain. Of course, the other room was a bedroom (with a bed that felt like a hospital bed having both the feet and head in the up position) and believe it or not between the two rooms was a full sized bathroom, but, there was no running water.

Outside of the cabin was a rain barrel which was filled regularly (trucked from a spring) and then the heating of water on the wood cook stove procedure was followed. There was one improvement over our cabin at the Native Institute. A plug could be pulled and the water disappeared down the drain instead of having to be hauled outside.

There was no electricity. Actually the cabin had a regular furnace in the basement, running water and electricity but they were all turned off for the training period.

The months at Chilanko Forks were like a second honeymoon for Chuck and myself. Mornings consisted of classroom sessions in Indian culture and religion; methods of breaking down communication barriers and testimonies of veteran missionaries. During the afternoon hours, the men had practical training in wood-cutting, first-aid, hunting, and cutting meat, horse shoeing and how to pack a horse with supplies, etc. The women took care of household chores during the afternoon hours. Some afternoons

24

Chuck and I visited in Indian homes but evenings and weekends were our own.

After a summer of never being alone, always surrounded by people, it was a pleasure to be by ourselves. Chuck and I got to know and enjoy each other again.

Not only were we never alone during July and August, but, with the need of finishing so much work before fall, often our days were ten, twelve and fourteen hours long. We began to irritate each other. It had reached the point where it seemed to me that no matter what I said angered Chuck. Since conversation never was very easy for me (which I attribute to being without peers so much of my childhood life) I lost all desire to talk to my husband. Then my silence irritated Chuck, so it seemed whether I talked or remained silent, I angered my husband. Naturally, I was hurting and felt between 'a rock and a hard place.' Often I would look at Chuck and think 'the last time you kissed me was the last morning you went to work at Boeing.'

But our training program was also a healing program for the two of us and seemed a way of escape from some of the pressures we had faced the previous months.

With Chilanko Forks being so far away from a city and stores, we were told to bring all our food staples with us when we came to Boot Camp. (This planning of food stuffs was needed for training, since some missionaries located in Alaska can only order staples once a year. These staples would come to their village up the Yukon River by barge in August.) Then once a month, we would go to town to get some fresh vegetables and meat.

We did not have very much promised support, but, did have enough money to purchase all our staples and some meat and vegetables to take to Chilanko Forks with us in September. One month, while in training, we received only thirty dollars support and had no meat left. The other people in training, unbeknown to us, learned about this and one noon when we returned from classes there was a surprise package of meats sitting on the table. Some of the missionaries invited us to their homes for dinner. How thoughtful of them to share their supplies with us. These acts proved again how the Lord cares for His own through His children.

Chuck and I had been in our little hilltop home only a few days when we had two little Indian visitors; girls of about six and eight years of age. A half hour after the girls came, their mother arrived. The mother could not speak English but could understand most of what we said. The girls had learned English when they went to first grade in school.

In Indian culture, conversation is not important, unless of course, you have something important to say. So, the girls would answer any question we asked but, most of the time, all would just sit silently enjoying each others company, but feeling no need to keep a conversation going.

This first meeting, we all sat quietly for about two hours and during this time, I served refreshments. Then one of the girls asked, 'You go to the store?' It was their polite way of asking to be taken to the store because, of course, if you were going to the store, you would not mind taking them along. We did not mind, so gladly took them. This was the first of many such visits and a love for these people sprang up in Chuck's and my heart .

Up until our first contact with Indian people had taken place, Chuck or I had never met or spoken to a native person before. We found them to be a very shy and quiet people most of the time. But, learned that when drinking alcoholic beverages, they turned into a violent people.

The mill at Chilanko Forks would give three day weekends after payday (every other Friday), because, they knew that the native people would be sleeping off their hangovers and not come to work on the third day.

When welfare checks came to those not employed, a great part of the check was used for drink.

During this time, the Indian people would often get into fights with knives or guns; or else someone would pick up a piece of firewood and hit the other person over the head.

At these times, the native people would usually come to the missionary for help. The missionary sometimes could care for the injury in his home. Other times, he would need to drive the injured person fifty miles to a nurse operated first aid station. Sometimes the person would be so severely injured that they would die before help could be reached.

The mode of transportation in this year of nineteen seventy, for many natives in the Cariboo, was still horse and wagon. Since the closest general store was about fifteen mles from Chilanko Forks, it was quite a time consuming ride by wagon.

Sorry to say, many of the small general stores in Indian country charged outrageous prices for their products, which is why the missionaries went the hundred and twelve miles into town for their groceries. There were times, too, when an Indian paid for their groceries with a welfare check and received no change when they should have gotten change. The older, non-English speaking, unschooled people did not know the difference.

In the fall, many of the native families moved out of their log homes and set up fish camps by the lakes in the area. There they would catch and dry their winter supply of fish.

Since the Indian's means of transportation was so slow the missionaries would drive the five, ten or fifteen miles out to the fish camps and bring those interested back to church for Sunday or evening meetings. Chuck and I gladly filled with native peoples, the good seating capacity of our travel-all.

Nights were now down below freezing and the plastic seats of our vehicle were like ice. One such night, we picked up a large family by the lake to bring into a Sunday night service. An elderly lady sat down beside me. As soon as she sat, she bowed her head and softly said 'cold'. That was the only English word I ever heard her speak.

Every four or five days the rain barrel needed to be filled. Two men would drive the truck eight miles and fill the three hundred gallon tank on the truck with water and return to fill the barrels. Men would take turns doing this and Chuck and Jess Tanis (one of the missionaries) often teamed together to do it.

A beautiful sunny afternoon, right after lunch, Chuck and Jess left to fill the water truck. I was cleaning our little home, a constant occupation, because the mill produced an ash which seemed to settle on every surface with a gritty substance. Not thinking of time, until everything was cleaned, including the floors (which were linolium and needed to be hand washed), I noticed that the air coming in the window had cooled. My watch said that it was near four o'clock and the men had not returned with the water yet. So, I went over to Alta's (Jess' wife) house and asked if she didn't think the men were long in returning? Alta and I thought we had better go check, so started out in her car toward the spring. We only drove the car about a quarter of a mile when we saw the two men walking toward us on the gravel road.

It was Chuck and Jess. They had filled the truck at the spring and then the engine refused to start. The two men had walked the eight miles home.

The truck became famous for refusing to start. One other time when Chuck and Jess were out in it, this time a wood getting detail, the engine konked out. Again the men had to walk many miles. Some of this time they had to walk through dense brush.

For years afterward, every time Chuck and Jess got together one or the other would say 'Hey, remember that walk?'

One of the other trainees was Stoney, the Indian who led the wood detail when the youth group came up to Chilanko Forks. Stoney is an Alaskan Indian who attended the Arctic Missions high school and Bible School in Alaska. The last portion of the senior year in the Bible School curriculum is an internship program with some arm of the mission. That was Stoney's purpose in being at Chilanko Forks in March. Now he was in training for full time service, like the rest of us, and was to become a Bible teacher at the Native Institute.

Some evenings the mission men, plus the trainee men, plus native men would get together and play basketball, volleyball, or baseball while the women sat together, did handiwork and from time to time chatted. Then naturally, refreshments would be served and once in a while the refreshment would be home made ice cream from the excess cream the missionaries cows gave. How delicious!

One evening, when the men were playing basketball,

Chuck came down from a lay-up and Stoney's elbow made a sounding contact with Chuck's ribs. They were cracked and Chuck was uncomfortable for a month. He was able to keep up with the training except for chopping wood and the other trainees (especially Stoney) kindly helped in this area.

There are no street lights at Chilanko Forks, but, usually they are not needed because the sky is brilliant with stars and moonlight. Often when Chuck and I strolled back from the fun nights we would walk gazing up because of the beauty. But, if the night was cloudy the paths would be pitch dark. A darkness that we had never experienced before. There were wild animals around also (including bears) and their sounds, especially coyotes, could be heard on the night air.

A cloudy, extremely dark night was stepped into, following one of the sports nights. Chuck and I slowly picked our way home when, just apparent to our vision, loomed a big black figure. We stopped and stared naturally thinking of a bear. Then we realized that it was a horse and had a good laugh.

On a special evening a Christian film was shown and the little public school house was packed to see it. A gentleman in the Cariboo makes this his ministry. He travels from Indian village to Indian village showing his Christian films. Such a thing as films of any kind are not seen in remote areas. Not even television is to be had. So, this is a treat and a drawing card for native people and the gospel is given.

Then one Sunday each month a missionary couple traveled to the reserve of Chezecut. The distance from Chilanko Forks to Chezecut was not more than sixty miles but took about three hours to travel because of the very bad road.

Chuck and I were asked to accompany the missionaries, Ken and Louise Lobdell, one of the Sundays that they planned on going to Chezecut. We left after the morning service and drove for a while then stopped to build a fire and have a doggie roast. After bumping and jolting along a two rut road, we arrived at Chezecut around three o'clock.

A message had been sent ahead of our arrival so as we drove from cabin to cabin the people were ready to squeeze into the van for the ride to the school house.

A very shy, gentle looking, elderly native man was one of the passengers who squeezed in the seat in back of me. He looked at me as if he recognized me (we had never met before) and started to say something then changed his mind.

During the meeting, Louise was telling the story of the 'Wordless Book'. As she reached the part where Jesus dies on the cross to forgive our sins, I happened to glance at Bobby Billy (the elderly gentleman) and tears were pouring down his cheeks; but, he didn't respond to the invitation.

Later, I learned that Bobby Billy was the most powerful witch doctor in the Cariboo. When I heard this the hairs on the back of my neck stood straight up and I often wonder what it was that he was going to tell me, but didn't.

Ken and Louise went to visit a native family a few days after our trip to Chezecut. The native family lived in a remote meadow. As Louise was sitting in the living room she looked through the doorway into the kitchen and there she saw a mountain lion laying by the door. She wanted to scream and run but sat quietly wondering if it was alive. Time passed and the animal's head began to nod which assured her that the animal was alive.

All the native people kept watching Louise's face. They had shot the lion and left it outside with its head propped up to freeze. Right before the Lobdell's walked in the front door someone brought the frozen cat in the backdoor to play a joke on Louise. As the animal thawed its head nodded. The whole native family thoroughly enjoyed Louise's discomfort and everyone had a good laugh when they explained what they had done.

Two highlights of the training time were two gospel team trips to two different reserves. Missionaries and trainees practiced several days with accordian accompaniment. Then vehicles were packed with tents, cooking equipment, wood stove, sleeping bags and clothing.

Anahim Lake, a hundred miles further west, was the first stop of our trip. The tents and all the equipment were set up right by the beautiful lake. After a good nights sleep we relaxed, went hiking and enjoyed the scenery for a day.

One unusual experience for most of us was the 'out'. Before, we all had used outhouses but there was no house at the lake. In a little brush, facing the lake was just a board with a hole in it. Each one of us had to sing or whistle when occupying the 'out' so others would know to stay away. All the men slept in one tent and the ladies in another. The ladies had the air tight wood stove for heat.

Fortunately the weather remained clear, so we were able to cook outside and eat on picnic tables. It was a relaxing and enjoyable time.

Our evening meeting was held in the Native Community Hall. There was a good turnout and everyone seemed interested in the music, the testimonies and the message. One of the favorite songs of the gospel team and of those who listened, was a medley of songs,

> Isn't He Wonderful, Wonderful, Wonderful?
> Isn't Jesus My Lord Wonderful?
> Eyes have seen, ears have heard, it's recorded in God's Word,
> Isn't Jesus my Lord Wonderful? [3]
> Wonderful, Wonderful, Jesus is to me,
> Counselor, Prince of Peace, Mighty God is He.
> Saving me, keeping me from all sin and shame.
> Wonderful is my Redeemer
> Praise His name. [4]
> Precious name, oh how sweet
> Hope of earth and Joy of Heaven
> Precious name, Oh how sweet
> Hope of earth and Joy of ---[5]
> Heaven is a wonderful place
> Full of glory and grace
> I want to see my Saviour's face

---

3. Peterson, Op. Cit. P. 264 (Chorus)
4. Compiled by N. A. Woychuk, Making Melody, St. Louis, Mo 1960 p. 23.
5. Peterson. Op. Cit. page 88 (chorus)

Heaven is a glorious, Heaven is a wonderful place. [6]
But until then my heart will go on singing
Until then with joy I'll carry on
Until the day my eyes behold the city
Until the day God calls me home. [7]

One husband and wife on the reserve were Christians, but the rest of the people living there did not know the Lord. The gospel was politely listened to that evening but there were no decisions for the Lord.

The camping equipment had been packed before the meeting and we all headed for our vehicles and home as soon as the service was finished. The weather had turned bitter cold and by the time we arrived home the temperature had dropped way below zero farenheight.

Our cabin had been without heat for over twenty-four hours and was like an ice box. Windows had a sheet of ice on the inside and the two rooms plywood walls had frost halfway up (inside). Chuck and I thought since it was after midnight we would just pile up our sleeping bags on top of our beds covers and climb between the sheets (then start a fire in the stove in the morning). For about an hour we laid in bed half cold.

The two cats that we had brought to Chilanko Forks with us (instead of leaving them for someone to care for at the Native Institute) knew where it was warm and kept crawling down under the covers with us. For the hour we stayed awake half cold, every five minutes we would pull the cats out and from around our feet, and immediately they would turn around, and creep under the covers, then on down to the bottom of the bed.

Neither Chuck nor I could stand it any longer, so, he got up and started the wood stove. In a short time the cats settled into their usual spots by the stove, the chill

---

6. Compiled by Ernie Rettino and Debby Kerner, Kids Praise, Maranatha Music, 1981.

7. Compiled by Ezra H. Knight and Jack W. Taylor, Sing and Praise Hymnal, Zondervan Corporation, Dallas, 1976, p. 92.

was taken off the cabin and the two of us dropped into sound sleep.

A few days later the weather moderated some and the gospel team travelled to the village of Nazko, about seventy-five miles north of Chilanko Forks. But by road, we had to travel approximately three hundred miles to get there.

Again we camped by a beautiful lake. This time on the property of a Christian rancher and his wife, where we were able to use their bathroom facilities. No 'out' this time.

The Nazko reserve had not had much contact with Christians and never before had had any experience with a gospel team. Again an evening meeting was held and there was a good group in attendance. But, halfway through the meeting the lights went out (someone had deliberately turned the light plant off). In the hall there was a lot of shoving and spitting upon the gospel team members by the natives. Our hearts were sad that these people did not want to hear about the saving grace of the Lord Jesus Christ.

One of the teenagers involved with the shoving and spitting was a young man by the name of Samson. For some reason the Lord particularly burdened my heart for him.

I often would remember Samson in prayer. Anytime someone from Nazko mentioned his name, my ears would perk up to hear the news.

Samson never showed any interest in things of the Lord, even after a missionary couple was placed in Nazko to minister.

After several years, Samson committed suicide. He was doomed to spend eternity in hell. It was a heartbreak for me.

Thanksgiving was a fun time. Each missionary family living at Chilanko Forks and those in training contributed some food toward a meal together. I had found several packages of blueberries (in the mission freezer which had been donated to the mission) and made four blueberry pies for dessert.

Pauline, and a young man she was friends with by the

name of Denny Mengle drove up from Seattle to spend the holiday with us. The temperature had now reached minus forty-five and we had some snow on the ground. Pauline and Denny had a trip north they will never forget since neither had ever experienced such extreme weather conditions before.

Charles and David came over from the Native Institute. It was a great few days to have so many of our family members together.

Patti could not make it home for the holiday since the college she was attending was down in California. She did spend the holiday with my parents who now lived in California. They called us by phone to greet us and cried through the whole conversation.

Calling such a number as Chilanko Forks - four- K (the home number of one of the missionaries) is a very exasperating experience with confused phone operators. When they finally reached us the noise crackled loudly on the many party lined phone and everyone sounded very far away. Mother and Dad also thought we were being deprived and going through a hard time. Tears of concern are very precious but Chuck and I did not feel deprived and we were having a great time.

A few hours each day during the holiday, the men spent working on our travel-all. With it s age and the extreme cold weather, half the time it would not start and the other half it would stop after it had run for a short while. Working in minus forty-five degree temperature around metal was very hard on Chuck's, Charles', David's and Denny's hands.

We all had a good time chatting and getting caught up on the news.

Charles and David told of how, after they had shortly arrived at the Parkins' home, they were undressing for bed with little John-John in the bedroom. All of a sudden, John-John ran out into the living room and grabbed his Daddy's hand saying 'Come, come'. John-John pulled his daddy into the bedroom and said, 'Look, they're one of us.' He was so happy to have two more males in the house and felt no longer outnumbered with two sisters and his mother.

Our two boys became acquainted with the ranching families who lived around the Native Institute. Also, a trapper and his son who lived about fifteen miles further into the 'bush'.

Charles and David visited in the home of Slim Dolven and his nineteen year old son, Tom. The cabin was several miles off of the gravel road and the Dolven's went in and out to the road either by horse and wagon or horse and sleigh. The comfortable log cabin they lived in often smelled of fresh baked bread by Slim who was a good wood stove baker. Slim usually served 'jar meat' with the bread plus potatoes and onions. 'Jar meat' is home canned moose meat and very good to eat.

Both Charles and David wanted to share their faith with the Dolven's. Tom said the only time he had ever heard of Jesus was when his mother read to him the story of Ben Hur. Tom had never learned to read or write.

This friendship that had begun with Charles and David continued on with all of our family as long as we remained at the Native Institute. Sad to say, neither Slim nor Tom ever felt the need for a Saviour through that time.

The first week of December was Chuck's and my last week of training; one day of which was to be in Arctic survival. Each trainee was to go out into the woods with one match to build a fire and then build a lean-to with pine branches.

Snow was thigh deep and the temperature was minus fifty when we woke the day of our survival trip. So, the class waited until the afternoon when the temperature had risen to minus forty-five and the sun was shining beautifully.

The mission had special Arctic clothing which they had purchased from the Army. We all put this clothing on and were surprised at how heavy it felt. Regular winter clothing was what we usually wore to walk from house to house or to church but this would not be protection for any length of time at minus forty-five or fifty degrees.

A van took us all out into the woods and we each had to make a separate path through the snow to a spot that looked good to build a shelter.

The lower twigs on the pine trees are always dead

this time of the year. To start a fire you break these twigs off and make a nice little pile in a spot where you have scooped most of the snow away. I had reached this stage and was ready to strike my one match when I looked over to where Chuck was located. He was waving to me and yelling. So, I plowed through the snow to him and found out that he had lost his glasses.

As Chuck had passed a low branch on one of the trees, the end of the branch ran under the side-piece going to his ear and flipped the glasses into the snow. They had sunk down and could not be seen. We searched and searched but the glasses could not be found. Finally, I saw in the snow the impression of a faint circle and we dug there. The glasses were found and the mark I had seen was the spot where the ear piece had gone through.

Chuck returned to building his fire and I returned to mine. We both were unbelievably cold and the heat felt good when the twigs were lit and the branches added. Then, the job of collecting pine boughs and forming some protection from the cold was accomplished.

By dusk, each trainee had finished and we all headed back to the van. Three lessons had been learned by all.

1. That complete exhaustion comes quickly from heavy clothing and plowing through deep snow. An exhaustion beyond any we have ever known in our life before.

2. In extreme cold, kidneys partially take over the purification that pores had previously done. Bladders become exceedingly full in a very short time.

3. If from exertion you do perspire the perspiration freezes to your skin underneath winter clothing making it possible to freeze to death more quickly.

Our training time was over. We were glad to travel back to the Native Institute and settle into our little cabin with Charles and David.

Now all four cots could be put in one room and in the kitchen area a stuffed rocking chair had arrived (on loan from the Parkins). It got to be a joke each night after supper to see whether Chuck or one of the boys would reach the chair first to claim it. I was not eligible because I had time during the day to occupy it. If the person occupying the chair had to leave it for some reason; immediately another person would jump into it and the first person had relinquished his rights to the chair for that evening.

Beautiful white snow had built up to about a foot in depth around our cabin; winter cold bit at our noses and Christmas Carols were on our lips.

We were surrounded by Christmas trees and would not need to purchase one for our little log cabin. All we needed to do was chop one down for our personal use. Such a concept was so new that Chuck and the boys couldn't restrain themselves and not only did they cut one down for inside our cabin but also four trees to sit by the four posts on the front porch of the cabin.

All of our Christmas tree ornaments were in storage in Seattle but that didn't hinder our decorating the tree. We made little ornaments to tie on and strung popcorn. It was fun and we enjoyed looking at our trees.

Around December twentieth we made our never to be forgotten travel-all trip to Seattle. (There waiting for us was the letter from immigration stating that we were to report for an interview right after the New Year.)

Pauline had been using our car to travel each day to college. Right then we traded vehicles with her. We felt that in the north, we could be stranded and even lose our lives with such an unreliable vehicle as the travel-all. Hoping that the travel-all would run better in a warmer climate and with the knowledge that help was much more available, if there were problems, in the Seattle area, we made the trade.

After a good nights sleep, Pauline, the two boys, Chuck and I climbed into our Chevy and headed south to California for the holiday. Patti was waiting at my parents home for us to arrive.

We experienced a temperature change of one hundred degrees. From minus thirty-five at the Native Institute of Canada to plus sixty-five in Los Angeles.

Charles and David went into the heated pool at the apartment house where my parents live right after we arrived. A lady who lived in one of the apartments right by the pool called down and asked 'Did you boys fall in?'

No one in California went swimming when it was sixty-five degrees. The woman thought that was too cold! The temperature felt like summer time to Charles and David.

The holiday was very enjoyable with many family members gathered together. My brother and his family, also my sister and her family visited, since they too lived in California.

Patti received an engagement ring this Christmas. Jim Ritter, her fiance, was one of the young people who went with the college and career group to Chilanko Forks in March. The two had met on that trip, corresponded since, visited each other several times and both felt that they were the correct choice for each other.

## Chapter V

A few days after the first of January our immigration interview was scheduled at the border station between Washington and British Columbia. Several hundred Christian's prayers were pointed toward our ten-fifteen a.m. interview time.

In our excitement about the interview, Chuck and I were busily chatting and did not realize that we had passed the turn off for the border station that we were scheduled to be at by ten a.m. We didn't see our mistake until we pulled up at a different border station.

Fortunately, we had started early, but we didn't know if we could drive the extra miles in time.

There was a straight duel road between border stations in Canada but the border guard would not let us into the country. So, we had to turn back through two lane, slow traffic roads and wind our way over to the other border crossing arriving at one minute to ten.

Again, the immigration official went through the point system and the interview came to an end with the same conclusion as that in Prince George six months before. Chuck did not have enough points for landed immigrant status. The official asked us to wait outside for a few minutes. We waited about fifteen minutes and he called us into his office again and said to us, 'While it is true that you do not have enough points to enter Canada, I have the authority to overrule this decision. Since I feel you will be a benefit to my country, I give my approval for your entry.'

The power of prayer was very evident that day in January nineteen seventy-one. Neither Chuck nor I could ever doubt where the Lord wanted us to serve. Chuck could not change his age, education or work experience but the Lord could impress an official with our worth and allow us to become landed immigrants in the country where He wanted us to serve.

Chuck and I were in the immigration office just about an hour and from there headed north arriving back at the

Native Institute in time for Charles and David to return to school without missing any days.

Shortly after we had gotten back to our little two room home we heard that several Christian ranchers from the village of Nazko (where we had been for one of our gospel team trips) had contacted Gene Parkins and asked if someone from the Institute wouldn't be willing to come out and conduct Sunday services.

Since Nazko was just about fifty miles beyond our home, Chuck said that our family would be glad to go.

The road from the Institute to Nazko was much worse than the road from town to the Institute. It was, in some spots, just one car wide. Some grades were extremely slippery if the weather was at all icy and you had to go through a mountain top pass that at times had snow or mud slides depending on the time of year. We had many a harrowing experience on that road with temperatures at minus thirty-five to minus fifty degrees but the Lord brought us safely through. One good thing about Sunday driving was that we didn't need to worry about meeting any logging trucks. It was their day off.

Each Sunday morning we would leave home around ten o'clock and arrive at the Nazko school house about twelve-thirty. The ranchers wives would have a potluck dinner ready for us. Following the dinner the service would be held. Everyone felt a special blessing during the worship time so far away from any urban area.

Dusk in central British Columbia in the winter months started around three-thirty p.m. and we would arrive home from Nazko about four p.m. A long day for one worship service but we felt it was worth every minute.

One Sunday Charles had a special school assignment and stayed home to complete it. I asked him to have supper ready for us when we got home. He was to put the meat in the oven around three-thirty p.m. Well, he heated up the wood cook stove, and heated it up, and heated it up. When we arrived home, the front door of the cabin was open and smoke was pouring out.

The meat had shrunk to a two inch charcoal encrusted lump. We ate it anyway but many times since, Charles has been kidded about his cooking expertise.

Our family made this trip to Nazko during January,

February, and April. Gene Parkins took our place in March and May. Then the summer of nineteen seventy-one a young couple was placed in Nazko to minister to the native needs and also fellowship with the Christian ranchers.

Early in February a thaw came and then a freeze. This repeated several times and soon we had icycles hanging from our cabin roof to the ground. They were beautiful. Ice also started to build up on the roof. When it reached a foot in thickness Chuck went up on the roof and chopped blocks of it off because he was fearful of the weight.

Chuck and the children had put a new roof on the cabin before we had gone to Chilanko Forks in September, because all summer when a shower came we needed buckets to catch the drips all over the cabin. Despite the new roof, the melting snow had somehow found a spot to come in and our one log bedroom wall had little streams of water cascading down. The leak was spotted and plugged which settled the problem.

Once a week we would travel to town for groceries. By now the road to town had snow piled six feet high at its edge and in many spots the road was just one vehicle wide. The curves and hills held many blind spots.

Gene would turn his short wave radio on when we left the driveway of the Native Institute of Canada. Every time we went to town Gene would hear a logging truck driver say over the short wave 'a Blue Chevy just went into the snowbank at mile so and so'. That was us.

Since in many places there was not room to pass a logging truck and they did not head for the snowbank that meant that we were the lucky ones.

The logging truck would keep on going but the driver would radio the next logging truck coming in either direction who would slow down when he approached us and be able to stop and pull us out.

One time a logging truck about a half mile behind us saw us go into the bank and the driver tried to stop to help but was too close to us and his wheels locked. The load of logs slid on the ice. The logs just missed the side of the car where I was sitting and swung over the hood. Chuck was standing in front of the car and just seemed mesmerized watching the logs come toward his head. Just as they were a few inches from him he had the presence of mind to duck and the logs passed over where his head had been. The truck driver got his rig under control and didn't try to apply his brakes again. We had to wait for the next logging truck but that didn't matter, Chuck's life had been spared.

Chuck went looking for and found some left over lumber from the previous summer to build bunk beds and a double bed in our little cabin. We put our sleeping bags on top of the wooden bed frames and this gave us more space than four cots side by side.

By now, I had developed some physical problems in using the outhouse in such extreme cold. So, we purchased a portable toilet and Chuck built a little cubicle between the double bed and the bunk beds. There was room in the little cubicle for the wooden wash stand with its plastic wash bowl on top. I could now wash without the men being banished to another room and visa-versa.

Chuck also found two old lawn chairs from which he used parts to make a bench for extra seating space. We were all a little more comfortable.

The pump in the well by our cabin had frozen solid while we were away at Christmas. But that didn't make too much difference because the boys just went to the Parkins home to fill the milk can, instead of the well. We were also invited to use the Parkins tub for our baths.

Due to the possibility of their cesspool becoming too full, the eleven people on campus were only allowed to take one bath a week. Gene put a piece of masking tape about 3 inches from the bottom of the tub and no one was to fill the tub above the tape. We had quite a time kidding about the tape and also joking with each other about being cold after a bath. Some local people thought that a layer of dirt helped to keep the person warm.

One morning David went to fill the milk can with water. It seemed like a very long time had passed and he had not returned home. Then we heard what sounded like a call and Chuck went out to investigate. David had slipped on a piece of ice and was laying by the gate to our front yard yelling, 'My leg is broken, my leg is broken.' The heavy loaded water can had landed on top of his leg when he had fallen.

Since Gene had a station wagon, David was lifted into the back of Gene's vehicle where he could lay straight and be taken into the Quesnel hospital. Fortunately, his leg was not broken but badly bruised and sore for several days.

Later in February Gene and Helen were asked to speak at meetings down in the states. So Chuck and I volunteered to care for their children. As it turned out Nancy and Vicky were asked to stay with schoolmates in town. That meant we only had John-John to be cared for and the girls beds were available for use by Charles and David.

For a week it was sheer pleasure to sleep on mattresses and enjoy for a few hours each day (when the light plant was on) electricity.

One of the most enjoyable pleasures for me these seven days was to be able to play the Parkins' piano. Music was missed by Chuck, David and Charles, and myself because it had been so much a part of our lives. With the furniture still down in the states, we could not listen to our phonograph nor could I play my piano.

An excellent battery operated radio had been given to us, but only one station was available. Quesnel's programming from six a.m. to midnight was just country and western music with the exception of one half hour each day when 'Back to the Bible' was on.

Several times a day we would listen to the Canadian news. The country and western music would follow and after a few minutes we could stand no more. A void was felt in our lives in the area of music.

Helen had several of the 'Favorite' song book series and each day of the week that we spent in her house, I would play through one or another of her song books.

One of these times, I came across a song I had never heard before. The words to 'Follow Me' were especially meaningful. At first, I could not sing the words because they expressed the cost my Lord had experienced to give me Salvation. Every time I tried to sing a lump would come up in my throat. After time passed I could sing the words to 'Follow Me'.

'I travelled down a lonely road
    and no one seemed to care,

The burden on my weary back
  had bowed me to despair;
I oft complained to Jesus
  how folks were treating me,
And then I heard him say so tenderly:
'My feet were also weary
  upon the Calvary road,
The cross became so heavy,
  I fell beneath the load;
Be faithful weary pilgrim,
  The morning I can see --
Just lift your cross
  and follow close to me.'

'I work so hard for Jesus' -
  I often boast and say -
I've sacrificed a lot of things
  to walk the narrow way;
I gave up fame and fortune--
  I'm worth a lot to thee!
And then I hear Him gently say to me:
'I left the throne of glory
  and counted it but loss
My hands were nailed in anger
  upon a cruel cross;
But now we'll make the journey
  With your hand safe in mine -
So lift your cross
  and follow close to me.'

'O Jesus if I die upon
  a mission field some day,
It would be no more than love demands -
  No less could I repay,
'No greater love hath mortal man
  Than for a friend to die' --
These are the words He gently spoke to me:
'If just a cup of water I place within your hand,
Then just a cup of water is all that I demand.
But if by death to living they can Thy glory see,
I'll take my cross and follow close to Thee.'   **8**

---

8. Singspiration Music, Songs Everybody Loves, Zondervan Corporation (Grand Rapids, 1963) p. 2.

In private or in public, no matter how many times I sang this song, the words remained precious to me.

When we first returned to our little cabin in January I wondered what would keep me busy. The place was so small that keeping it clean required very little time. But washing clothes, cooking and doing dishes continued to take longer than in an electrified home. There was preparation for the music at the Nazko meetings and preparation for an evening Bible study that I was teaching. I was also embroidering a large tablecloth and napkins, in my spare time, which had been purchased with the thought that sometime in the not-too-distant future we would need a wedding gift for Patti and Jim.

There was much more to keep me busy than I had previously thought. But, still there was a break from everyday teaching. It was something that the Lord, in His wisdom, knew I needed.

The second building that had been built during the summer now became occupied by a young couple by the name of Dan and Ginger Work.

Dan grew up in Pennsylvania, his wife in Washington state and they met in Alaska while counselling at Arctic Missions summer camping program.

The Work's had gone to boot camp a year ahead of us and then on deputation for a year. Dan was scheduled to become the mathematics and science teacher; Ginger the art and home economics teacher when school opened. Both were now finishing off the interior of their home.

The mission's procedure was for a couple to go out on deputation following their training. Since we did not want to leave our boys again it was decided that Chuck and Stoney Nicklie would go on deputation together and I would stay home with the boys.

Chuck went down to the states in March to arrange meetings at churches that had shown some interest in Arctic Missions. The churches were located in Washington and Idaho and the mission had supplied Chuck with the contacts. Stoney and Chuck then went out in May and June to the previously arranged meetings and shared with the people the ministry that the Lord had called them into.

It was true that we had very little support but, oh how

the Lord proved that He was able to keep us during that time.

My shoes were worn out and in the 'missionary barrel' sent to the Institute was a brand new pair of loafers, my size, which I wore every day for a full year before they showed any sign of wear.

We were able to afford very little meat. Gene came to Chuck one day and said, 'I'll give you half of the moose that I shot if you'll help me cut it up.' Chuck immediately became a butcher. Neither Chuck, Charles, David nor I had ever eaten moose before living in Canada. The meat is delicious! Our table now had roasts, ribs or stew every night until summer.

Not only our needs were being met but even our wants. One morning as I was baking cookies I felt sorry for myself because we could not afford nuts to put in to them. Two weeks later a couple from Oregon drove into the Institute's yard. These people had jars of canned goods and fifty pounds of walnuts they had gotten from trees in their yard. They thought maybe we at the Institute might enjoy using these things. How right they were!

When Chuck and Stoney left home at the end of April, they went in our Chevy and I had permission to use Stoney's car to go to town for groceries or if their was any emergency.

Charles had decided to try out for the schools spring Rugby practice. He had played on the football team down in the states and rugby was similar, but rougher.

One afternoon, I drove to town for groceries and then I went over to watch Charles at rugby practice. In between watching him, I was writing a letter to Pauline. In the letter I was describing the game and wrote, 'I don't know what position Charles is playing but he's standing at every play.'

After the game was over, Charles got into the car with me to go home. I asked him what position he played in the game and he answered, 'The coach thought since it was my first day it would be best if I just observed.' We had a good laugh at what I had written and my ignorance of the game.

Another trip I made to town was an emergency one.

Charles had been out in the woods getting some firewood when a guard on the chain saw fell off and part of the saw cut a deep gash in Charles' thigh. Fortunately another fellow was with Charles. He drove him home to me so that I could take him to town.

One afternoon I looked out of the back window of our cabin and there stood a cow. The snow was about thigh deep so I went to get Helen Parkins (the men were in town on business) to help me get the cow back to its owner who lived just about a half mile down the road. Helen and I huffed and puffed through the snow trying to edge the cow toward the driveway. The cow would then hop over the snow and go the wrong way every time. My boot would stay stuck in the snow and my foot would come out. That would leave me standing like a stork on one leg trying to get the other foot back into the boot to try to accomplish the feat of bringing both foot and boot out of the snow at one time. When this happened several times, all I could do was lay back in the snow and laugh. We did finally get the cow back to our neighbor.

Our neighbors were very interesting people. The cow belonged to Mrs. Paley, a widow who lived alone. Mrs. Paley came to the Baker creek area as a small child. Her parents were the first homesteaders in the area (In the early nineteen hundreds) where the Institute was now located. Her husband was a Hudson Bay salesman who took the goods out into Indian areas to sell. A very self-sufficient woman who continued living on her own in her log home after her husband's death.

At the lake, where we rented the cabin the previous summer, lived Fred and Else Tibbles and their youngest daughter Nancy who was in high school. Fred was the first child born in the Baker Creek area. Both the lake and the road that the Institute was located on were named after these people. Fred is a registered hunting guide.

A few miles from the Institute lived the Cooper family, Tom, Ann and their six children. Tom worked in Quesnel. Ann had been a teacher in a little one room school house twenty years before. The little log school house is just a short distance from the Institute, but all children now go into Quesnel for school, so it isn't in use.

Beyond the Coopers another few miles lived the Jones family, Eve, Perry and their son. The Jones' were a ranching family who had immigrated from the states.

Out close to where Tom and Slim lived there was a ranch owned by Dude (an early settler) and Margaret Lavington. Dude was a well known person, as his life was mentioned in several biographies about ranching in Cariboo country.

Some of the old time ranchers and trappers wives were 'mail order brides'. Women who came from eastern cities to marry and work beside men they had never met before. A concept, that to me belonged a hundred years ago in history, not in the twentieth century. Yet here I was meeting them and appreciating them.

These were our neighbors and people whom the Lord put a burden in our hearts to reach for Him.

Helen Parkins, Ginger Work and I would visit from time to time with the community ladies. Each month the ladies on Tibbles Road, Lavington Road and Nazko road met together to plan community functions and socials. The meeting was held in a different home each month (home choice was determined by the last name, going alphabetically) and refreshments were served.

Also, once a month the men and women would meet together for community business and a social time in the community hall located between the Institute and Mrs. Paley's home. For most of the socials we would join in with the other community members, but there were a few that we preferred not to attend.

There was a good rapport between those living at the Institute and the people in the community. We helped each other at haying time, loaned equipment to each other and visited. They would patiently listen when we shared our faith but felt no need for it in their own lives.

All winter long a little white ermine would appear on our cabin's front windowsill to gaze in during suppertime. Once in a while he would find a hole to come inside, run around the room and out again. However, he had not been seen for sometime. Evidently, Spring was making its approach. To replace the ermine were hundreds of birds nesting around our cabin. Each morning we would wake to a concerto of chips and chirps. Then another sound became a daily occurrence; the honking of Canadian geese flying north.

Some days would be comical. The geese would be honking and flying north when a snow shower would come. The next thing we knew they would be headed south honking all the time. Then the snow shower would clear and again they would be heard overhead headed north.

Other signs of spring were all around, also. That is mud, water, frost heaves and frost boils. The snow had melted, causing mud, the creek had greatly overflowed its banks causing more mud. Frost boils and heaves were all over the road to town and had to be avoided or else the car would sink down into the soft soil of the boil to stay. It was easy to break a spring, shock or axle on the heave.

With spring also came the planning for summer construction. Our home with a dorm wing was one project. The other project was to build a small two bedroom cabin for the use of any native family in attendance at the Institute.

The warmer weather brought the arrival of individuals or youth groups to help with all the work that needed to be done.

In the middle of the night, around three a.m., a knock came on our cabin door. Charles went to answer it and I heard him say 'Just throw your sleeping bags on the floor'.

At six in the morning, I walked into the kitchen to make breakfast and there on the floor was wall to wall young men. I had to step over about fifteen of them to get to the wood cooking stove.

During the years that followed many a person would leave Quesnel in the afternoon, make a wrong turn somewhere and drive for hours over logging roads before they would arrive at the Institute to knock on someone's door in the middle of the night.

In May, Chuck and I were able to attend Pauline's graduation from the University of Puget Sound and then the two girls came home with me to spend most of the summer. Charles and David moved onto cots in the third building that had the walls and roof up.

Three young men arrived the first week of June from Colorado, an older man from an eastern state and a native young man by the name of Vincent Yellow Old Woman from Alberta also had cots in the building with Charles and David. These men planned to stay the summer to help with construction.

One day, Pauline, Patti and I snuck down to the building where the boys slept and filled the seven cots with pine cones and needles. After midnight we heard the sound of hammers pounding on our cabin. Boards were swiftly nailed across the door and all five windows.

As I lay awake, I thought of the possibility of death by fire with no way to escape. Neither stove was burning and there was no way for such a thing to happen, except by lightning. So, I turned over the fear to the Lord and went to sleep knowing that early in the morning the door would be unsealed because breakfast was served at our cabin.

Tom Dolven rode his horse to the campus one morning and told everyone that there had been sightings of a Sasquatch in the area. David came to me and said, 'Wouldn't it be fun to fool everyone?' I drew a two foot long foot and David cut the foot out of a piece of plywood. Then he and Charles went looking for a muddy spot to make impressions of the foot in the mud. After they had placed several 'steps' a few of the toes broke off, but they continued putting a few more steps anyway.

Later in the day, Charles and David told Tom Dolven, the fellow from Colorado, Paul Cass (the older man) and a young people's group (who were peeling logs) that they had found evidence of the Sasquatch. All went out with cameras to take pictures of the footprints. Some noticed the missing toes and asked Tom, 'How do you account for that?' His answer was, 'Frostbite. It'll do it everytime.'

Everyone fell for the hoax and some people didn't find out till several years later that it was a joke.

I was headed to town for grocery shopping when the school needed a roto-tiller. I said I'd be glad to pick one up at the rental store.

When the salesman placed the roto-tiller in the back

of the station wagon, he couldn't shut the rear door. All the way home dust billowed up from the gravel road and in the open door. It covered me from head to toe. I looked like a walking grey cloud when I emerged from the car back at the school. Parkins granted me special permission to take a bath before my due time.

The high school youth group from our home church south of Seattle, Landgren Memorial, came up to help for two weeks. They were instrumental in getting the foundation and floor laid of our home to be. We had great fellowship for that time. How apparent the love and concern for our well being was expressed.

Summer was really here which meant swarms of thousands of mosquitos everywhere and everyone was lavish with the 'Off' when going outside. But mosquitos weren't only outside, they were inside also. For the problem, coils of 'Raid' were burned and a blue hazy smoke floated around the cabin rooms day and night. No-see-ums presented a problem outside. This was a very minute fly that anesthitised before biting. Usually no one knew he was bitten until he felt a trickle of blood. About three days after the bite a small lump would develop and in another four days the lump would itch like fire. 'Off' was some help to prevent this discomfort but often the No-see-ums flew up under a sleeve or shirt tail or pant leg and did his dirty work where no 'Off' had landed.

School for the young people going into Quesnel closed the last week of June. Both Charles and David had found jobs for the summer. Charles at a resort on Tibbles Lake and David on two ranches.

At this stage of David's life he thought he would like to be a veterinarian. He had always had a love for animals and now being around cows and horses as well as household pets increased his interest.

David worked part of the summer at Dude Lavington's ranch. Here he had the unexpected taste of assisting a vet.

One of the cows developed trouble calving and Dude decided that he had better take the cow to Quesnel for medical care. The hour and a half trip was very difficult in the back of a pick-up truck for the animal. When the vet saw the cow he decided to do a cesarian section right in the back of the truck rather than moving her.

She was lying on her side. After the doctor removed the calf, the cow's intestines spread all over the bed of the truck. The vet said, 'Come on, we have to shove them back in.' So Dude, David and the vet pushed and pushed until everything was back inside for the vet to sew her up. Sorry to say the calf was dead, but the cow recovered.

When Chuck returned from deputation it was apparent that the Lord wanted us to continue relying completely upon Him for finances. We only had ten dollars more a month of promised support.

The Parkins went to Alaska for three weeks in July. Chuck, the girls and I moved into their home for that time. Two of those weeks, my parents were up to visit and we were so happy to be in a large enough place for them to stay.

Pauline and Patti were such a help with all the food preparation. We usually had fifteen to twenty people to serve at each meal.

The first time that Patti used the oven in the Parkins' house she turned the gas on and walked away expecting the automatic pilot light to light it. After she had mixed the cake she realized that the oven wasn't hot and lit a match to light the oven. What an explosion occurred! Patti was not hurt but she was frightened. Several windows had blown out and a few more cracked. The oven did not have an automatic pilot and she had never used an oven like that before. Aside from this one problem, food preparation and clean-up went much quicker with a propane stove and automatic hot water heater.

Three weeks quickly went by. It was like pealing back a century to return to the old cabin to live. This did not last long because the next project was stringing electric wires from the light plant and putting in ceiling fixtures and wall outlets. Then a little propane cook stove (that just fit in one corner of the cabin) was installed. The old wood cook stove was removed. We now had more room around the table and the work load became lighter.

Again the pressure of always working and always being surrounded by people began to take its toll.

The youth groups that came were filled with great exuberance and some young people rose at dawn, four thirty a.m., and worked until dusk, eleven p.m. Some young people would even drive their cars up to where they were working and turn the head lights on to work on into the night. How we did appreciate this help and enthusiasm but most groups were only with us a week or two. We who lived at the Institute had to help supervise this all summer and our own stamina wore low.

Each youth group had their own devotional time in the morning with their counsellors. We also encouraged them to have part in the mid-week prayer time and Sunday services. Staff and guest ladies met on Tuesday mornings for prayer and devotions.

Some evenings, teams were formed (Native Institute personnel versus guests) to play baseball. Other nights, some would go swimming or fishing. Once a week a hot dog roast and bonfire was planned. Usually on Saturday afternoon a hike was planned to a pretty little falls about five miles into the woods from the Institute. Or some groups planned a day trip to visit the famed gold rush town of Barkerville. These activities usually included every one at the Institute.

Chuck and I also felt the need to reach out to the young people in the community. We planned a sports evening each Friday followed with a devotional time and refreshments. Usually eight to ten Baker Creek young people plus some Institute guests would meet at the Community Hall for the evening of fun.

For some break from the pressure, each afternoon for an hour or two, I would go to a quiet place (about a half mile from the cabin) in one of the meadows and sit on the bank of the creek. There I would drink in the beauty around me and on the distant hills. A quiet peace and the presence of the creator of this world would fill me. Chuck also discovered this spot and it became known between us as our 'quiet spot'. In the eleven years at the Institute, it was visited many times either alone or together. The blessing we each received from the 'quiet spot' always filled our need.

If possible, August became more hectic than the rest

of the summer had been. Pauline returned to Seattle to look for work. Patti returned to California to get ready for school. Their excellent help to me was gone. Then Patti wrote and said that she and Jim had decided on being married the end of the month. To top it all off, our home was just about ready for occupancy and that meant that our furniture needed to be moved from Seattle.

We did manage.

The moving and storage parking lot looked like a flea market. We had furniture and boxes everywhere. Some things were loaded into a U-haul to go to Canada. Other things were packed into a pick-up truck and taken to a friend's home to be kept for a few days until Chuck and the boys returned from Canada. Then these things were to be taken to California in a U-haul trailer for the use of our daughter Patti and hubby to be, Jim. The third load of furniture and boxes was also to be stored at a friend's house. These were to be kept until Pauline was ready to set up housekeeping.

In mid afternoon the truckload for Quesnel, B.C. was packed so Chuck and the boys hopped in and headed north. Twelve hours later the truck was droning out the gravel road toward the Native Institute of Canada. It had gone down a steep hill and was grinding away to climb another hill but not succeeding. Charles and David shouted over the noise 'down-shift Dad, down-shift'. Chuck responded 'why, I'm going down hill.' It was good they only had a few more miles to drive when tiredness had so dulled the senses.

Later that morning the truck was unloaded into our apartment and after a good nights sleep Chuck, Charles and David were ready to drive south to return to Seattle.

The day went by slowly but without any major problems until about one hundred and fifty miles from Seattle climbing a hill, the truck died. On a three lane highway the bulky U-haul truck blocked the southbound lane. Cars whizzed by on the center passing lane and the northbound lane. Chuck and the boys sat on the curb waiting for someone to assist them.

An R.C.M.P. car went by and Chuck was upset when the officer didn't stop. In a few minutes a civilian car stopped and Chuck made a remark about the R.C.M.P. car not stopping. The response from the car driver was 'I'm an R.C.M.P. officer'. (Evidently the first car had radioed the second driver.) Even as Chuck was talking to the officer he heard a familiar voice say 'What's the problem, Chuck?'

A family who had been helping at the Native Institute of Canada had left for home hours before Chuck and the boys had headed in the same direction. The Holden family had taken the scenic route south so they arrived at the spot of the stranded vehicle late at night.

In a few minutes a truck came along and pulled the U-haul truck to a scenic view area at the top of the hill. Now that it was off the road, the Holdens headed south with Chuck and the boys packed in with them. Chuck left the truck keys at the R.C.M.P. office in the town of Hope. Then all went to eat breakfast at midnight. Chuck and the boys had missed supper and were starved.

The U-haul company was notified about their truck's location and its problem, the next day. Now all were ready to head south with the U-haul trailer to Patti and Jim's wedding in California.

Following the week in California we returned to the Native Institute of Canada and found our new house in much the same condition as the Parkins' and Work's houses were when they moved in. Plenty of interior work yet to be finished but it was good to be home and fairly well settled just after Labor Day.

The house was shaped like a 'T' with our living quarters being the cross bar. We had a large living room, kitchen and dining area, bathroom and two bedrooms. The leg of the 'T' was the dormitory wing consisting of five bedrooms (for two students each) and a bathroom-laundry combination. We were now ready for students.

## Chapter VI

The Native Institute of Canada was designed as a high school and Bible school for the Indian and Eskimo peoples. Missionaries working with native peoples felt that the work of discipleship was hindered due to the lack of education of the people that they were working with, hence the need for the school was conceived.

Out in remote areas every Indian reserve had a one room or larger public school located close by. This school went to grade eight. Anyone going to high school had to board in town to attend. But, most Indian young people dropped out of school before the eighth grade since attendance was not compulsory and several other factors discouraged learning.

1. All teaching was done in English. Many native children spoke only their native language and heard English for the first time in first grade. Barrier number one!

2. The learning process on the reserve was to produce a graphic functional mind. Their thinking was literal and pictorial. White culture teaching is to produce a conceptual abstract thinking process. Barrier number two!

3. In Indian culture adults stayed up late and slept late. Usually the children did the same. The adults would not be up to get the children up to go to school and many days of school would be missed. Barrier number three!

4. Living in one or two room cabins with ten or twelve other family members was not conducive to good homework or study methods. Barrier number four!

5. Many times the teaching quality was poorer in the remote areas. Urban school boards would seek out teachers with better ability and qualification, leaving the less gifted teacher to find only schools in remote areas open for employment. Rustic, remote, lonely living is not a drawing card for most teachers. Barrier number five!

In their reserve area schools, some children were passed from grade to grade, never learning each year's studies. Other children were not passed but soon reached the stage of a large age difference with their classmates. Native children would become discouraged and felt inferior because they could not keep up with the class. Parents did not feel that education was a big benefit to reserve living. Therefore, many left school in the fourth or fifth grade.

Anyone who did complete eight grades would be discouraged by their parents from going to the city to finish school. The parents did not want their children to leave home. Even though the parents were aware of the problems on the reserve, they felt there were greater problems in the city. Problems their children could not cope with. Also, those students that did go to the city for studies ususally did not return to the reserve to live.

Native children raised in, or close to an urban area, seemed to have a better school record. Some of the barriers were not present and others were lessened. Most urban area natives finished the eighth grade and once in a while one would go all the way through twelfth.

Then there were natives who were older and had been out of school for several years who felt the need to finish high school.

A Christian school curriculum had to be designed to meet all of these needs. A high school age young person needing to complete grade school work; a high school age young person doing high school work; people in their late teens or twenties who had been out of school for several years needing to finish high school; high school graduates wanting Bible School education; adults in their thirties, forties, and fifties who wanted Bible School training. Above all the educational needs there was a great need for love, compassion and patience.

These babes in Christ needed instilled in them the desire to learn, the benefit of learning and good study habits.

Each student that applied had to be recommended by a missionary or pastor. They also had to answer form questions and write a statement about when they had accepted Christ as their Saviour.

The Lord sent us exceptional young people to work with the first school year. They were:

Mary Angus, a Thompson Indian who had known the Lord for a few years and who had lived in a missionary's house part of a year. Mary was a teenager who had finished eighth grade in the public school and came to the Native Institute for grade nine. Mary lived in one of the dorm rooms of our home.

Larry and Ellen Antoine (Mary Angus's sister) were Thompson Indians who also had known the Lord for a few years. Larry had finished high school and came to the Native Institute of Canada for the first year of Bible School. Ellen had left school and wanted to take high school courses (in Canada this is known as upgrading).

Larry arrived at the school in May. True classes weren't to begin until September, but Larry had had some trouble with the law and the village missionary thought it would be best for Larry to be away from the influence of his friends. So he arrived on campus to help during the summer with building and all the other chores.

Just before Larry came he had served some time in prison. While he was doing this his wife Ellen, with their little daughter Lucy, went down to Vancouver to take a course in child care. The course didn't end until late in June, so Ellen and Lucy didn't arrive at the Native Institute of Canada until almost a month had passed from the time of Larry's arrival.

Ellen and Lucy flew up from Vancouver and Pauline drove into Quesnel to pick them up. All Pauline could talk about, when she got home, was how beautiful Ellen was and how cute Lucy was. The beauty was not only in Ellen's appearance but also in her gentle, sweet personality.

Everyone fell in love with big, jovial Larry, his attractive wife and their adorable little girl.

One of the summer projects was the building of a cabin for this family. But it was not ready for occupancy when Ellen and Lucy arrived, so the Antoines were sharing living quarters with a missionary family.

It was at this point that I had my first real encounter with culture shock. Larry came to me and asked me if it would be all-right for Ellen and he to use my bed during the afternoon.

Such a request would be unthinkable in our culture. But the young people felt the need for privacy and in their culture there was no embarrassment in making such a request in such a manner.

I attempted at keeping the look of shock off of my face and told Larry that the bed was free for their use. Then I told Chuck of Larry's plans and advised our four children that Larry and Ellen were planning on taking a nap in our cabin and to make sure that there was no need to go into our two room abode during the afternoon.

We were all busily engaged elsewhere on campus from one to five o'clock.

The Antoine's cabin was ready for occupancy early in August.

Larry worked all summer. Even when it was time to get the hay in. This was an ordeal for him because he was subject to hay fever. With every bale of hay that Larry threw the tears flowed heavier down his cheeks. Being good natured he took all the jokes about a grown man crying.

Ellen had only been on campus a month when she decided to give the Parkins' dog, Princess, a haircut.

The Parkins had gone to town when Ellen went to work with the scissors. Princess was an odd shape for a poodle. She was thick in body and her legs were short. No matter what Ellen did, the dog did not look dignified.

Ellen left the premises and Princess hid under the sofa when the Parkins returned.

Sarah Antoine (Larry's sister) a Thompson Indian who had known the Lord for a few years. Sarah had lived with a missionary family while completing high school. Sarah came to The Native Institute of Canada for the first year of Bible School and lived in the room with Mary Angus in our dorm.

Art and Sharon Dick, Thompson Indians, and new Christians. Art came for first year Bible School and Sharon for upgrading. This couple resided in another one of our dorm rooms.

Lewis Holmes, a Thompson Indian and new Christian. Lewis came to finish high school. He lived in the second building with Stoney Nicklie.

Jeannie Hunlen, a Chilcotin Indian who had known the Lord for over a year. She came for upgrading but only stayed until Christmas break. She lived in one of the rooms in our dorm.

Gerald Tom, a Thompson Indian and new Christian. Gerald was forty-two years of age and had only attended a few grades of elementary school. He came to the Native Institute for Bible training but did not arrive until the second semester.

Gerald had planned on coming in September. He and Lewis Holmes were hitch hiking to the Native Institute of Canada when the car that they were in had a terrible accident. Lewis came on to school with his arm broken and in a cast but Gerald had more extensive injuries and had to remain in the hospital. When Gerald did arrive at the beginning of the second semester, he was on crutches. Gerald Tom lived in the house with Stoney Nicklie, and roomed with Lewis.

Bernie Williams, a Haida Indian who had known the Lord for a short time, came late in the second semester. Bernie was a foster child to white Christian parents, who were interested in and gave support to the Native Institute of Canada. She came to us for ninth grade and lived in our dorm.

Bernie's childhood had been spent on the beautiful Queen Charlotte Islands, off the coast of British Columbia.

60

She had been raised by her Grandmother. Then when her grandmother had died she had been placed in a foster home. By the time her present foster parents had her she had lived in many homes. She had had many unpleasant experiences. Bernie also had a constant yearning to return to the Islands. Naturally her personality was affected. She could be very pleasant but also very bitter and resentful. Her tongue got her into a lot of hot water.

One summer we visited the Queen Charlotte Islands. Their beauty was exceptional and the Indian villages well kept. The Haida artwork was everywhere. Fishing was great and seafood abundant. We could easily understand Bernie's yearning.

The students arrived a few days before classes began. One of these afternoons Sarah came to me and said she and Mary were having problems with homesickness. Walking to the lounge in the dorm section I prayed that the Lord would give me wisdom in how to deal with this problem.

Homesickness was a great problem in the life of native people because tribal people feel a loss when not near each other. They depend upon each other's presence for security and when away from the tribe they feel insecure.

We sat and talked for several hours during which time I shared off and on about my own loneliness. My loneliness for my parents and the desire to live close to them so we could visit with each other. My loneliness for my daughters and a desire to live close to them. Then I shared how I knew that the Lord had chosen me to be at the Native Institute of Canada to teach and counsel students. I told them how it was more important to me to be where the Lord wanted me to be than it was to give in to my loneliness. Then I shared how that it was important for them to be where God wanted them to be and how at this time in their lives God wanted them to be at a school where they could learn more about Him. We finished our time together with prayer.

My prayers were answered. Both girls were satisfied that the Native Institute of Canada was where they should be. Although I am sure that they were still homesick, they

never complained about it or gave up and went home because of it (which some students did in later years).

Dan Work injured his back before classes began and needed to go into the hospital in Quesnel. This meant that someone had to take over his classes. Chuck said he would teach the science class. Gene Parkins took the mathematics class. It had been a long time since Chuck had studied science so now each evening Chuck would study for the next day's lesson.

Because the road was so bad out to the Native Institute of Canada the doctor would not allow Dan to travel it after he was released from the hospital. The whole first year we were two teachers short. Dan, Ginger and their baby stayed in an apartment in Quesnel.

Besides the science class, Chuck's days were busy with interior finishing work in our dorm. Some of the plumbing yet had to be connected in our bathroom; closets needed to be built and doors put on the door frames; extra insulation needed to be stuffed in cracks between logs and the finishing strips put over the insulation. The flooring was just particle board and not finished. The ceilings also were unfinished wallboard with seams needing spackling, taping and finishing. There was plenty to do. Besides this, Chuck was kept busy helping to keep the plumbing and light plant functioning (a problem that increased as the weather got colder). Another job that was Chuck's responsibility was the purchasing of food and supplies for the school. The mission thought it would be a good experience for Chuck to have the sermon each Sunday morning, so he had the preparation for this during the week.

A door factory down in the states donated hundreds of imperfect doors to the Native Institute of Canada. They were used not only for their regular functions but for shelves, tables and other unusual objects. Each home also had beautiful kitchen cabinets that had been donated to the school. Some were oak and others mahogany. They were a pleasure to look at and use. The third building that had been built in nineteen seventy was converted into the school building with three big classrooms.

My classes were taught in our home. I taught French, guitar class, gave piano lessons and held choir practice. In Canada, French was a required subject in high school. No staff felt qualified to teach French and it was decided in staff meeting that since I had learned to pronounce the

language while taking voice lessons that I was the most logical person to teach the subject. I had studied Latin in high school (it was a recommended subject for people considering the career of nursing) and Spanish in college but learned to pronounce Italian, German and French for singing purposes. Each evening I joined Chuck in studying for the next days lesson. I needed to comprehend what we read or spoke in class. Records were available on the subject which helped a great deal.

Cooking was also my responsibility. All the students plus Stoney Nicklie and our family ate around the dining table in our part of the dorm.

Eating around the table was a new experience for some of the native young people. In the Indian culture people ate when they were hungry. Since people got hungry at different times food was kept prepared all day long and the individual just helped himself when he was hungry.

For many, the Native diet consisted of eggs and rice in the morning. Fish or meat, usually moose, plus rice for afternoon or evening consumption. Bannock, or fried bread as it is also known, was another food eaten regularly.

Our table menu included these foods. Fruits and vegetables were also introduced and usually liked. For many of these new foods we had what was called a 'no thank-you helping' which was just a teaspoon size serving to eat (being a school situation we felt the learning experience should include food).

Chuck, the boys and I had our first taste of Indian Ice Cream. It was made from an orange colored berry that was beaten until very light and frothy, then a little sugar was added. The substance looked like pink meringue and appeared delicious. What a surprise to our taste buds when the extremely bitter taste hit them. It was a flavor that no one in my family ever developed a taste for, but the Indian people could consume large bowls of the whipped berry.

My daily schedule went like this:

6:00 a.m. Light plant started and everyone got up
6:30 a.m. Breakfast (Chuck helped prepare)
7:00 a.m. Charles and David left for school
8:00 a.m. Students started classes

64

9:00 a.m. French Class
11:00 a.m. Watch little Lucy (both parents had class this hour)
12:00 p.m. Lunch
3:00 p.m. Guitar class three days, voice class two days
4:00 p.m. Piano lessons
4:30 p.m. Piano lessons (Charles and David came home)
5:00 p.m. Piano lessons
5:30 p.m. Dinner
7:00 p.m. Choir practice
10:00 p.m. Devotions, lights out and sleep

In my spare time I did my housekeeping, food preparation, baking and counselling. The students took turns doing dishes and were responsible for keeping their rooms and bathroom clean. Mary graciously often helped me with the cleaning of our living quarters.

Much fresh fruit was given to the school at the beginning of September. Some was eaten fresh, but the quantity was so great that I needed to can most of it before it spoiled. Being a city girl, I had never canned anything before so had to read how to can and then ask people who had canned some questions to make certain that I knew what I was doing before starting. By this time, some fruit had already spoiled.

On a Saturday afternoon, the fruit was sorted and the spoiled fruit put in a box outside the kitchen door to be taken to the dump on Monday. The good fruit was successfully canned.

Dinner was at noon on Sunday. After Chuck had carved the roast I said, 'Why don't you throw the bone out in the back yard to the dog?' I opened the back door and saw a big furry animal at the bottom of the steps. My first thought was, 'My, that's a funny looking dog', then I realized what it was and screamed, 'there's a bear out there'. The spoiled fruit had drawn her. I slammed the door shut and with me holding it shut, Chuck tried to open it to see the bear. David ran into the bedroom to get his gun. (He had just gotten a bear tag the day before).

In the meantime, the students were all sitting in the living room. Some were fearfully clinging to each other and others were yelling. Most native people greatly fear bears and respectfully stay a great distance away from them. They know and have experienced the power of the bear and many native people believe that the bear's spirit is a supreme spirit. While our native young people were all Christians, a lifetime of fear cannot be sluffed off in a short time.

David shot three times. The bear continued to stand with one shot in her head and two in her chest. She then turned and ran under the house (the skirting around the base of our home and the dorm was a job that Chuck yet needed to do). After Dinner Chuck and David went under the house and found the bear dead. We had meat for our table for several months.

The black female bear weighed about three hundred pounds and proved to be quite tender. Since it was close to hibernation time when Chuck skinned her, she had about three inches of fat on her back. It was a surprise to find that the grease on Chuck's hands from removing the bear's fat clung to him for several days even after many washings with soap and water.

Dried fruit was another donation to the school. The students enjoyed munching on the dried apricots, apples and pears. I also stewed the fruit to eat at mealtimes. Then I made apple pies. The crust was delicious but being a 'green city slicker', I had put the dried apples with sugar, cinnamon and butter into the pie crust without pre-soaking the apples. I thought the apples would soften from the baking and was very wrong. They became very tough and brittle. Of course, the pies were for a special occasion (American Thanksgiving) when the village missionaries came and had a turkey dinner with the Native Institute of Canada's staff.

The polite missionaries never said a word. It was several years later before I realized my mistake and realized how terrible the pies must have been.

Bernie's foster parents owned a potato farm and they offered the school a good supply of potatoes if the men would help with the harvest. Three students and one staff member went down to help for a few days. We stored the potatoes in the last room of the dorm, which was unoccupied. They kept well until the really cold weather arrived and no heat got to the back room. We could have cooked them frozen if we had known, but the first inkling of their frozen condition was after they had thawed and moisture seeped out under the door into the hallway. Everyone felt bad at the waste.

One evening little Lucy stood up in her high chair. I told her to sit down and heard Stoney say to me 'aren't you going to let her learn?' I was much surprised at that question and it wasn't until much later that I realized the full impact of what it meant.

The philosophy of Indian culture is that a child learns by doing. They are rarely corrected and not told to not do something.

If a child stands in her highchair and gets hurt falling to the floor she will know not to do it again. If a boy touches something hot and gets burned then he will know not to touch something hot again. Etc.

Sorry to say many little lives are lost and many children disfigured because of this philosophy.

The school kept a few beef cattle for student consumption. One was slaughtered and taken to town for butchering because the staff had no free time to do it. The beef looked good when we took it into town, but we received back hamburger, stew meat and tough pot roasts. The meat was a disappointment and everyone felt that the butcher had switched meat on us. In future years the butchering was done on campus.

With these provisions supplied, the cost for each meal per person averaged thirty-three cents the first year of school.

Chuck and I went to town each Friday afternoon to purchase staples (flour, sugar, etc.) some fruit, vegetables and paper products. We would usually have three or four shopping carts to push up to the register. Even though it was a weekly occurrence the cashier's eyes would get big and she would say, 'What are you going to do with all this food?' Even at the end of eight years we were still greeted with this question.

One week toilet paper was on sale. Chuck approached the cash register with several cases. The clerk's wide-eyed question was 'What are you going to do with all this toilet paper?' He wanted to reply 'it's just a week's supply' but restrained himself from saying it.

Shortly after classes began, I started to have great pain in my shoulder joints, hip joints and the base of my spine. The pain became excruciating every time I moved day or night. But it seemed each time I visited the doctor there was no pain. The doctor started to take all kinds of tests and X-rays.

One visit to the doctor my knuckles appeared dark and he said that this was a sign of a rare disease. When the test result for this disease was returned it was negative.

The X-rays showed no arthritis and there was no swelling at the joints, a sign of arthritis.

Test after test returned negative. One test had to be sent to Vancouver for processing and the vials of blood were dropped and broken on the train south. Another delay and the blood had to be retaken. It was at this point that I began to realize that the testing and diagnosing was not going normally. I began to suspect Satanic opposition and began to apply Scriptural principals to the problem but did not exclude the physicians medication because the Lord is able to give the doctor wisdom in his diagnosis.

After three months of tests and various medications, some of which I proved allergic to, the doctor said, 'Every test has shown negative but since the problem is in the joints it will be diagnosed as arthritis.' He put me on a new medicine for joint inflammation. Then the doctor arranged for physiotherapy treatments because I was losing mobility of my neck and arms.

Now I needed to fit into my daily schedule, a half hour of rest, a half hour of arm, neck, leg and back exercises and a half hour walk. This fit into the after lunch time slot. (These exercises, plus medication, plus resisting Satanic forces began to lessen the pain. It was a year before the medication and exercises could be stopped and six years before becoming fairly pain free.) How thankful I was that the Lord gave me the strength to continue all phases of my ministry through the pain.

Baker Creek community always has two big events in October, held at the hall. The first Monday of the month is Canadian Thanksgiving. The Native Institute of Canada staff and students joined in the feast of turkey, goose and **pot-luck dishes, the Saturday night before the holiday. Our** students only attended this celebration the first few years of the school when the student body was small. As the student body grew, the staff felt that it was unfair to the community to bring twenty or thirty big appetites to the dinner.

Thanksgiving is held on the second Monday in October in Canada because the harvest is usually over before the last of August due to the long days of sunlight for growing. Frost often comes late in August and the crop would be lost if farmers waited that late to harvest.

When the Thanksgiving holiday was first instigated, travel to celebrate with other family members would have been very difficult later than October. It would be easier to stay home than travel in the bitter cold and snow. Road conditions and the warm vehicles to travel in today do not present the problem that was experienced in past years.

A Halloween party on the Saturday night before Halloween was a fun time at the hall for all. Adults and children donned costumes and were judged for funniest, prettiest, most unusual, etc. Then candy was handed out to the children. Door to door 'trick or treat' was not a usual practice because of the distance between homes. Lastly, a fireworks display was held outside. People stood out in the freezing night air to watch the display without any thought of cold.

Each student enjoyed getting themselves costumes from the old clothing assembled in the missionary barrel. The girls in the dorm not only fixed themselves up but assisted Charles in getting ready for the party. He had found some ladies clothes to fit and the girls had put up his hair in very tight curlers and teased it so that he had an 'Afro' hairstyle encircling his head and they applied make-up to his face. He wore a mini-skirt and padded sweater. Charles' long legs and high heels presented a figure that could not be overlooked.

David dressed as a horror creature with a ghoul mask to top it all off. Chuck and I dressed as a couple going to a military ball. Chuck wore an evening gown and high heels. He stood majestically over six feet tall and my five feet, no inches clothed in an old ROTC uniform carefully supported Chuck's arm like any good escort would. We won the most unusual couple costume prize.

As Chuck, Charles, David and I in costume started to walk out of the Native Institute of Canada's long driveway, a propane truck started driving in from the gate. The driver was new and the closer the truck approached us the bigger his eyes got. He never smiled when he asked us where to go to fill the propane tanks and his face would have made a classic snapshot of, 'What have I gotten myself into now?'

The school did have a difficult time proving its credibility in town. Several years before the Native Institute of Canada began, another group had proposed a Bible School not too far from our property. This group's leader had approached the churches in town for backing. By nineteen seventy-one this group had proved disappointing to their backers and were considered a hippie commune. Our school was often mistaken for the other group and it took quite a few years to overcome this stigma.

One way the problem was overcome was through churches in town needing a fill-in pastor and asking one of our staff members to come to preach. One church was between pastors and either Gene Parkins or Chuck preached there every Sunday for nine months. Then another church experienced the same problem and a rapport was built up. So we became known and respected. It took longer for the non-Christian community to accept our credibility. If either Chuck or Gene took a female student to town for doctor or dentist appointment and was seen walking on the town street together they could see disapproval in the passerby's eyes. From then on we had to be very careful in who went to town with whom, not wanting to give any reason to cause a misunderstanding of our morals.

Lewis had a bad toothache. We took him to a dentist in Quesnel and Lewis came out of the office with four teeth pulled. We were horrified and had more lessons to learn, this time concerning medical treatment for Indians. If a native lived on a reserve, he had tooth care coverage by the government. If he was away from the reserve, the only thing the government would pay the dentist for was the pulling of a tooth unless paperwork was filled out on exactly what needed to be done and then sent to the government for approval to have the work done.

This we did not know and the dentist had performed the only thing for Lewis that he would get paid for. After this experience, we learned the proper process. Oral care for the students had to be planned well in advance because of the length of time the paperwork required and dentists were usually booked three months in advance. It was not a simple thing to get a toothache taken care of.

Fortunately, medical care for Indians was paid for by the government whether they lived on the reserve or off of the reserve. But, we found that some doctors were indifferent in their care for Indian people, others were prejudiced and did not have an open appointment time for the native person. It took time to find a physician that was reliable for the student's physical problems.

Pastor Landgren, from our church in Washington, plus his wife, Lenora and a couple (John and Iris McAdams) from the church flew up from Seattle for a visit. The McAdams owned a plane and John flew the four up. They landed in Quesnel and Chuck picked them up to bring them out to the Native Institute of Canada. The thirty-three mile drive from town took four hours because the road was especially bad and the muffler on our car fell off. Chuck had to find wire to put the muffler back on. A conversation subject of the Landgren's and McAdams' for many years was the fact that it only took a few minutes more to fly from Seattle to Quesnel than it took to drive from Quesnel to the Native Institute of Canada.

Both women in this party had artistic gifts and spent a good part of their time sketching students faces or the picturesque buildings, especially the barn. The two men relaxed, hiked or helped Chuck.

As evening approached, the night before the McAdams' and Landgren's were to return to the states, horses could be heard snorting outside our building.

Someone had forgotten to close the driveway gate. Whenever this happened horses usually came on the campus. April through October was open range for the ranchers cattle. Cows and horses grazed along the road these months and whenever they found an open gate they went inside. Since we did not like being kept awake at night by the horses snorting or their neck bells ringing outside our bedroom window, nor did anyone like walking in the dark through animal deposits on the lawn, the men usually rounded them up and herded them back out to the roadway and closed the gate.

This night was no exception. Chuck, Pastor Landgren, John and Charles went out to get the horses out to the road. When the job was finished the men realized that Charles was missing. They didn't know where to look until Pastor Landgren heard a moan. Charles did not know that a pit had been dug in back of our old cabin for a septic tank. Running in the dark, he did not see the hole. The three men found Charles laying in a heap in a corner of the twelve foot deep pit.

Just a month before this night round-up, Charles had had a knee operation for a torn cartilage (torn during a rugby game). When he had fallen in the hole he passed out from the pain. We all feared that Charles' knee surgery had been damaged but thank the Lord, that was not true.

A few months after Charles had his knee surgery, David tore his knee cartilage while skiing and he too required surgery.

While David was coming out of his anesthesia, Chuck and I sat alongside of his bed. Every few minutes David would sit up and say, 'See that man over there? He's from Barkerville!' and David would point to an empty bed.

School friends (male) visited while David was still not quite conscious and David would either do the 'Man from Barkerville' bit or else he would pull the blankets off before we could stop him to show his friends his bandaged knee. The reason we attempted to stop him from showing his knee was because the hospital gown only went to his waist.

For quite some time David's friends had a good time kidding him about his actions.

The surgeon who performed Charles' surgery was in the room as soon as Charles came out from under his anesthetic and had Charles raise his leg. The doctor then left orders that in a few hours Charles was to get out of bed and walk around the bed. Charles' recuperation was very quick.

David's surgeon did not follow this procedure. David was operated on a Friday and the doctor did not come to the room until Monday. The muscles would not respond and David could not lift his leg. My youngest son had three very exasperating days before there was any response in his leg. It took David a much longer time to get off his crutches and walk. There were a few spiritual lessons about calling on the Lord for help, about patience and about the Lord's timing that David needed to learn and he learned them through this experience.

To keep the big dormitory plus our apartment heated was a continuing process. Early in September we were given a large franklin stove. It was placed between the dining area and the living room. On the cool days and frosty evenings the stove kept the chill off of the living area.

When October arrived, more heat was needed and an air tight stove was installed at the other side of the living room. One advantage the air tight had over the franklin stove was that when loaded at night it would burn all night and there would be red coals in the morning to add wood to.

By November, everyone realized that this heat would not be sufficient for the colder weather. Chuck and Gene designed a big barrel stove to go under the house. It was completed and placed under the house early in December. A grate was placed in the center of the building where the dorm wing joined the living area for the rising heat. This kept our living area comfortable but the bedrooms still remained very cold.

Fortunately, many quilts had been donated to the school by church missionary societies. Most beds had four to six quilts on them. We were all toasty warm in bed (except for my feet) no matter how cold the weather became.

The greater heat was much appreciated but now we had to go outside and under the house to load the logs in the furnace. Often we had to have two of the stoves burning. Chuck and the boys usually stoked all the stoves. I usually did it once a day, late in the morning, when the men were teaching or attending class.

The barrel stove did not hold the coals all night and some extremely cold nights Chuck had to set the alarm clock every two hours to go fill the furnace so that the water pipes would not freeze. (This stove was used for two winters and then an oil furnace was installed in its place with duct work going to all the rooms. How comfortable we all were when this took place.)

The Christmas season approached and packages started coming in the mail. Mail arrived once a week, on Fridays, to a mail box five miles from the school. What a surprise it was to see each package's contents and cost listed on the outside. Customs required this declaration and all gifts under fifteen dollars came to us duty free. This was the first Christmas both Chuck and I knew what everyone was receiving. We did manage to keep the information from the boys.

After the students left for their Christmas holiday at home, our family planned a trip to Prince George to do our shopping. Chuck, Charles, David and I rose early to a fifty degrees below zero temperature. On our way to the car, I glanced down the furnace grate and saw the floor boards around the furnace glowing a bright red. They were on fire! The boys and Chuck grabbed up the grate, turned the furnace fan off and sprayed the burning wood with foam from a fire extinguisher. Our trip was slightly delayed but how thankful we were that the fire had been seen. Otherwise we would have returned home from Prince George to charred ruins.

We had a beautiful pine tree (which we had cut down a short distance from the dormitory) nicely decorated and the four of us had a lovely time together opening gifts. This was the first year the girls were not with us for the holiday. They were missed. Patti and Jim remained in California. Pauline stayed in Seattle. This Christmas she received an engagement ring from Denny Mengle and they planned a June wedding.

Every previous Christmas day a part of our tradition

was serving chocolate candy. We had none this year because we did not have the money to purchase any and if we had had the money Quesnel had no shop in which to purchase homemade chocolate candy. The thought kept crossing my mind how we would miss this one little thing. Then between Christmas and New Years from several different people we received a total of ten pounds of candy.

How delicious it tasted and how hard it was on my waistline. (The added weight was much harder to take off than it was to put on.) Through this experience, I was reminded once again how the Lord constantly fills our cups to overflowing.

Art and Sharon Dick were late returning to school from the Christmas break because little Joshua Dick arrived while they were home. We now had a few weeks old baby in the dorm and what a good little fellow he was.

As I had anticipated the new arrival, I was concerned about the possible lack of sleep due to a baby crying in the night. Knowing that my system usually came down with the flu or a bad cold when I didn't get eight hours sleep; also knowing how the school was already short staffed and losing another teacher through sickness would cause a problem gave me good grounds for concern. This need never have been because Joshua was never heard at night. From the beginning, Indian babies are taught to cry softly, (when they reach speaking age they are taught to speak softly).

Jeanie Hunlen was not allowed to return to school Her mother did not feel that Bible Study or education was important. Since Jeanie had several younger brothers and sisters and there was no father in the house the mother had placed much of the smaller children's care on Jeanie for quite a few years before she came to the Native Institute of Canada. The mother did not want all the responsibility she had to assume with Jeanie away.

This is a common custom in many native homes. What is assumed as parental responsibility in white culture is often passed on to other relatives in Indian culture (older children, grandmothers and aunts). It is assumed on the reservation when the child is playing outside the home that child care is everyone's responsibility and not one person's in particular. All the women and young girls care for whatever child is playing near them. Discipline problems are dealt with by the aunt for girls and by the uncle for the boys.

When the new semester began, Chuck no longer needed to teach science, as an Alaskan missionary, Barney Furman, who was on furlough, came to the Native Institute of Canada to help until the end of the school year. A young Eskimo woman, Lucy Coolidge came down from Alaska to help in the office and in the classroom for a few months. When looking at Lucy Coolidge, no one would know that she was legally blind. She was a good worker, her gentle manner and loving kindness quickly won students to her.

Barney will always be remembered for his inability to blow up a balloon. Every Friday evening staff and students had a game and skit night together. On the particular night of the balloon blowing episode, everyone was divided into two teams and formed two lines. Each person was given a balloon.

The game was played by the person first in each line running to a chair, blowing up their balloon and heavily sitting down on the swollen balloon to break it. When the balloon broke, they would run to the end of the line and the second person in line would have their chance. The first team finished was the winner.

Several people had to sit hard, two or three times before the balloon would break but Barney's (who was second in line for his team) problem was that he could not fill the balloon with air. Barney blew and blew all the time the other team was playing. His team lost but no one really cared because they had laughed so hard over Barney's antics, contortions and facial expressions in trying to blow up his balloon.

One very constant occupation of missionary life is letter writing. The volume was increased for me, many fold, compared to pre-missionary life. This aspect of the ministry was one that I had no previous concept of, nor any concept of the time that would be required to do all the writing. There were personal letters to family and close friends to be written. Once a month a prayer letter had to be written and sent to the home office to be printed and distributed to our five hundred plus prayer partners, another letter was composed each month and sent to the home office (with the prayer letter) to be distributed to the mission members for prayer. Letters were written to answer questions from churches and individuals, thank you letters were written for support received through the home office and gifts that came in the mail. The month with the most volume of letter writing is the month after Christmas. Cards with personal notes have to be answered; cards with gifts have to be answered and thanked. People who sent packages have to be thanked. What a blessed time of the year! What love is expressed! But what a busy letter writing time for each mission family.

Charles and David tried out and were selected for the Quesnel high school basketball team. Before they had not had much chance to participate in school sports because the school bus from Quesnel to the Baker Creek area left the high school at two fifteen in the afternoon. Sport practices were held after that time and the boys had no way to get home if they missed the bus.

A new ranch family (the Long's) moved just two miles from the Native Institute of Canada. Mrs. Long worked in Quesnel and drove home at a time when the boys would be finished practice. This kind lady offered to bring the boys home and they were delighted to now be able to stay for basketball practice the days that it was held.

Because of the great distance between towns when school teams competed the competitions were held on the weekends. Several schools would compete in a tournament which would have a Friday night game and two or three games on a Saturday.

Chuck and I were usually able to attend the games played in Quesnel and a few times we were able to attend some of the Saturday games in distant towns. The two of us were surprised at the lack of parental participation in viewing the games. Often we were the only mother and father at the game. When we lived in the states, the school games were well attended and we were surprised at the disinterest of parents in Quesnel. It pleased our boys for us to watch the games and we enjoyed being there.

A few times practice was late getting over and the boys missed their ride home. First they tried to hitch hike home but people travelling out our road after dark in the bitter cold were few. Then they decided to stay at friends in town when they missed their ride.

Thrice a day messages are broadcast over the radio for people without phones. The times they were broadcast were twelve thirty-five p.m., and five thirty-five p.m. and ten thirty-five p.m. Each time the boys did not arrive home in time for supper Chuck and I would stay up to hear the ten thirty-five message on our battery operated radio to make sure the boys were safe.

Message time was an important time and everyone at the Native Institute of Canada always listened to the noon ones. All the new babies arrivals were announced, (we learned about our grandson's arrival in April down in California through the message that was phoned by Jim to the Quesnel radio station) the deaths and funeral dates were announced plus who was to meet who at what time and anything else that people who lived in the bush needed to know.

One time the physiotherapist needed to cancel my appointment for my arthritis treatment. She contacted the radio station to send a message that came at the noon broadcast and it was read over the air 'To June Temple, to June Temple at Baker Creek, your psychotherapy treatment has been cancelled.' The announcer had goofed and everyone in the Baker Creek area had a good laugh. My good friend Ann Cooper said to me 'I always thought you were crazy and now the radio station confirmed it.'

Messages could reach us through the radio but our contacting someone from the school was more of a problem.

When it was necessary, Gene would use his short wave radio to contact a person who had a short wave radio. Then that person would put in a phone patch to the person in his area that was to be spoken to. The conversation was not two way; one person would say what they had to say and then say 'Over and Out'. Then the other person would have to say the same thing when they finished.

By the Baker Creek hall there was a public phone

booth that contained a radio phone. The process was the same only through the phone company operator instead of another short wave operator. The cost for this phone's use was quite high.

Before the end of spring nineteen seventy-two the British Columbia Telephone Company installed phone service as far west of Quesnel as the Native Institute of Canada. Each house on campus had its own phone.

We were on a party line with about twelve other parties each of whom had a different ring. Our personal ring was three longs and one short.

Chuck, Charles, David and I usually had a puzzled expression on our face when the phone rang. Half the time we could not tell whether the ring was long or short because the long wasn't held long enough. The other half of the time we were trying to remember whether our ring was three longs and a short or three shorts and a long.

Everyone on the line answered each other people's calls. Then came several days when somewhere wires got crossed and the phone rang solidly from morning to night for every party. The only way to get away from the ringing was to go outside. (Two years later the phone company installed a new substation and everyone received a regular dial phone. Now only five or six families were on a party line and each phone rang individually.)

In the evening after supper our family would have devotions around the dining table with the students. A different person would take turns reading Scripture each night. This would be followed with a prayer time.

After Gerald arrived second semester, when it came to his turn to read the Scripture he would say, 'I can't read too well.' and the Bible would be passed on to the next person. Gerald had a stuttering problem and found it difficult to read and speak. After a few weeks of not reading, Gerald decided that he would try to read when his turn came. When Gerald read the Bible the Lord kept his tongue straight and Gerald was able to read the whole passage without much difficulty. What a victory! It also became apparent as time went by that Gerald could give his testimony almost free from stuttering. This was a definite sign of God's power to Gerald.

Native people have a compulsion to seek out power. From centuries past through to the present day, because of their animistic beliefs, power is sought. Usually the power is that of some animal spirit. Satan used this belief. When an Indian receives the ability to do some extraordinary feat after praying to his spirit helper, his belief is reinforced.

A native gains the knowledge of who his spirit helper is by fasting and physical ordeals. The first animal seen after this rite is the spirit helper. It could be a dog, a horse, a deer, an eagle and many more.

Gerald's evidence in speaking clearly was the first of many events in the student's lives at the Native Institute of Canada that showed the power of God over ordinary everyday events and also over any previous spirit power.

Gene and Helen Parkins were invited to a Missionary Conference. This time John-John stayed with us instead of our staying in the Parkins home.

We had sandwiches for lunch and John-John left his crusts. Kidding, I asked John to look at all the student's plates to see if he could find any crusts. When he didn't find any I asked him how did he expect to get big like the students if he didn't eat his crusts. Without a word, John-John consumed each crust morsel.

The day after the Parkins returned Helen asked me what I had done to John-John. Naturally I wanted to know what she was referring to. Helen said, "At lunch he ate all his crusts without saying a word."

Little Lucy was a sweet little girl. Each evening when she sat in her high chair at our dinner table she would usually fall asleep sitting straight up. Sometimes during the meal when her hand, with a spoonful of food in it, was halfway to her mouth, she would fall fast asleep. Everyone would chuckle at this cute scene.

The hour of watching Lucy from eleven a.m. to lunch time had become more difficult for me. Early in the fall, Lucy had napped at this time so lunch preparation was no problem. Now she did not sleep at that time any longer and usually I would be busy preparing some food when I would realize that all was quiet and Lucy wasn't around. I would find her back in the dormitory tearing everything out of the student's drawers. 'Diplomatic counselling' or different forms of punishment did not solve this problem. I felt at my wits end and could not understand why the dear child could not be corrected in this and other problems that began to surface.

Several years later, it was learned that Lucy was epileptic and that she had some brain damage which caused learning disabilities. She was placed under medical observation for a few years before the right combination of drugs were found to control the problem. It is a shame that this hyperactive little girl did not have the benefit of these drugs during the time she lived at the Native Institute of Canada.

Teaching music to the Indian people proved very interesting and also challenging. The students proved eager to learn. Hymn singing and music in general was new to them; it was meaningful and enjoyable. Their musical heritage was the drumbeat, singing (a high pitched chant) and guitar music from listening to the country and western songs they heard on their radios at home.

The voice class lessons that I taught were on the basic fundamentals of singing. The student learned how to breathe correctly and how to produce sound from the diaphram. They were taught how to hum and what pitch, volume and tone quality were. Time was spent in diction and correct word pronunciation when singing. The girls quickly

developed sweet singing voices. Some fellows had difficulty because they sang everything an octave lower than the normal range; others sang partially monotone. When these problems were conquered the fellows also developed good singing voices.

For choir rehearsals the staff sang with the students. Since none of the native students could read music, I thought this would be the most effective way to teach harmony. Charles, David and Chuck sang base. Stoney and Gene sang tenor. The men students were divided by their vocal range and practiced with the staff to learn their parts. We practiced the same way with the girl students since Helen and one of her daughters sang alto. The other daughter sang soprano with me.

After the New Year through to May several churches in Quesnel and Prince George invited the Native Institute of Canada choir to sing at their evening services. Helen accompanied on the piano for some songs and Larry accompanied on his guitar for others. We even had a male quartet arrangement of hymns.

Following these meetings the remark was often heard, 'This is the first time I ever heard an Indian sing.' We also heard, 'This is the first time I have seen an Indian that wasn't drunk.'

The church people in towns usually had no reason to go out to the reserve where the native people are not drunk a good part of the time. Many native people came to town to drink. A drunk Indian person is often the only way that they are seen in urban centers.

All the students wanted to attend guitar class. In class, they were taught how to pick out melodies and also chord accompaniment. Some students enjoyed practicing and did it on their own. Other students thought they would learn to play by just attending class and not practicing between lessons. The latter student did not learn to play.

At our services I played a little chord organ for accompaniment and the guitar class would chord along through the songs. There was just one problem that developed. All the guitars had to be tuned before church because the chord organ was a small degree sharp. They also all had to be retuned before class to the pitch of my

82

piano. Since the student's ears had not developed enough to distinguish the tone difference the guitar tuning job was mine (after months of listening the students ears developed enough to tune the guitars themselves).

Practicing was not only a problem for those taking guitar lessons but also for those taking piano lessons. To practice was not a part of the native culture so the method had to be taught. It took me several years of frustrated teaching before I found a solution to this problem.

In the white culture parents usually made sure that their children practiced. A similar solution was devised for the students. At first at the Native Institute of Canada, two piano's were available for practice; later two more were added for use on campus. Each of these pianos were assigned to staff members so that they could follow through with certain students assigned to him (her) to make sure that the practicing was done.

When the student began taking lessons each year he (she) was given a practice chart with a space for him (her) to mark down the time he (she) practiced each day and another space for the staff's signature each day. Once the schedule became regular the students progressed well and I felt that the lesson had become worthwhile.

The piano lessons were held after classes. This time of day did not prove much of a problem the first few years but as the student body grew, I ended up having lessons every afternoon until supper and some days after supper. Supper preparation and dish clean-up became difficult. (This schedule was followed for four years after which time the students were released from classes to come for their lesson. Now late afternoon and evening pressure was no longer present. After the mid-seventies, more people became staff members of whom three were able to teach piano. All four of us had busy piano teaching schedules during the released time.)

Drum playing was never incorporated as a part of accompaniment for the singing or worship services. While rhythm and a beat are a natural part of native culture it was also a part of the rites of spirit worship. Some of the drumbeats were used to call the spirits. The information about this was not revealed to the white people and I did not know what drumbeats were used for this purpose. Each tribe had several lodges and each lodge had their own secret rite, therefore it would be impossible for even the students to know all the information concerning the drum beats.

Once we had a group of students attending a seminar in the city of Seattle. When the students came out of the meeting some of the Hare Krishna cult were on the sidewalk beating their drums. Several hours later when travelling home in our car one of the girls was very upset because she could not get the drum beat out of her head. She was very oppressed by the beat.

Chuck counselled her, while he was driving, about the power of the Lord Jesus Christ over Satanic oppression and then everyone in the car sang a favorite chorus:

In the name of Jesus, In the name of Jesus
We have the Victory.
In the name of Jesus, In the name of Jesus
Satan will have to flee.
Who can stand against that mighty
    name of Jesus Christ God's Son?
In that mighty name of Jesus
We have the Victory won. [9]

The girl was released from the sound of the drum pounding in her head. This part of her spiritual culture could not be thrown off except through the name of Jesus.

People living in a white culture would probably never have such an experience. Native people are drawn by the power of Satan to bondage by certain beats. Since I did not want this phenomenon to occur, drums were not used at the Native Institute of Canada.

Chuck, Charles and David planned on building a deck, to extend outside the living room door of our apartment, during their spring break. They had an enjoyable time working together and we all enjoyed sitting on the deck when the weather became warm.

One afternoon we were absorbing the sun and enjoying the view from the new deck when we noticed that the

9. Moe, Danny, Sing Out, Surrey B.C., Worldwide Ventures Publisher 1972, p. 266.

cows out in the meadow were headed toward the barn. The time of day was unusual for this to happen and we wondered the cause and scanned the meadow to see if anything unusual was in view. There on the edge of the meadow sat a wolf and the cows were heading for safety.

Those of us who lived in the Cariboo could say that this was 'the year of the wolf'. After dark their mournful howls could be heard along with the short yipps of the coyote. When late winter arrived the ranchers had to keep close watch over their cattle.

A neighboring rancher had a steer attacked by a wolf. By the time he had reached its side the steer had jumped into the creek and drowned. The meat was donated to the Native Institute of Canada and the students enjoyed the good beef.

Beef was the preference meat of the students who came from ranching country. And they ate every part of the animal. We ate parts that we as a family had not eaten before but there was one delicacy to their taste that we could not ourselves eat. The students called it 'cow guts' and that's what it was. The washed intestines were dipped in flour and fried. We were very happy that we were not on dining hall duty when 'cow guts' were served.

The coastal Indians preferred fish, especially Salmon. One student would bring from home, each time she returned to school, several jars of home canned salmon, which she would share with everyone.

We did not often have salmon in the dining room but usually each spring there would be a trout feast. Again there was a delicacy that we could not appreciate. It was the fish head. The coastal student would put the whole head in her mouth and the only thing not swallowed would be the jaw bones which would be neatly placed on the plate.

The school received a special gift and Chuck bought doorknobs for all the bedroom **doors**. They were installed while the young people were in school. When Charles and David came home they noticed the new knob right away and Charles let out a loud 'Whoo-ee, we have a door knob.' Everyone experienced such pleasure over such a little thing. Chuck and I remarked to each other later that evening how that when we lived in civilization we took so many things for granted. The boys would never have experienced joy over a doorknob when we lived in the states. Probably many city people would think we were real unsophisticated to have such happiness over such a minor thing but then they had never lived without doorknobs.

Some days I would be so busy that I would think 'the only way that I am going to get any rest is to get sick.'

The surprising thing was that very often, in ten days or two weeks I would come down with the 24-hour bug or a bad cold and have to stay in bed a day or two. Outside of the discomfort, I'd usually be refreshed and ready to take on the challenge. Even in illness I could see the Lord's hand at work.

Spring breakup of nineteen seventy-two finally came. All winter, snow had fallen almost daily. Since there was very little wind, the snow built up to five or six feet out in the meadows and around the buildings. But the snow packed down on the paths between the houses and school buildings by the staff and students walking. The malady of 'cabin fever' (a sense of being bound in the home; partly due to the quantity of snow) had been experienced in February and March. Now that we could walk where all the snow had once been piled the cabin fever was gone.

One day as I was taking a walk in the meadow I was pondering how it seemed that the presence of God was no longer close but seemed a million miles away. Here I was a missionary doing the Lord's work, yet I did not experience the closeness of the Lord in my daily life that I had felt before I came to the mission field. Then the Holy Spirit brought the verse to mind 'Be still and know that I am God' Psalm 46:10. I realized that I was never still, my schedule was too busy, yet I could not change my business. There was a need for more time in the word and prayer to solve this problem. I determined to take time in the morning to do this and chose right after everyone left for classes, when the house was quiet and I was alone. My devotions before sleep never stopped but the morning time became very precious and was the lift I needed to experience peace and joy through the busy day.

The words of the first verse of 'My God and I' came to

mind and became a blessing to me. I was constantly humming the tune or singing the words as I worked.

My God and I go in the field together
We walk and talk as good friends should and do;
We clasp our hands, our voices ring with laughter-
My God and I walk thru the meadow's hue;
We clasp our hands, our voices ring with laughter-
My God and I walk thru the meadow's hue. **10**

Every one of the living room and dining room windows in our quarters were angled so that we had a perfect view of the hills beyond the meadows. Daily as I would look out I'd be reminded of the Bible verse Psalm 121:1,2 'I will lift up my eyes unto the hills from whence cometh my help. My help cometh from the Lord who made the heavens and the earth'. The spiritually dry time began to abate. All of the Psalms became very precious. As I studied them they gained new meanings that I had never appreciated before.

Chuck and I were able to get a break from the busyness. The Basic Youth Conflicts Seminar was being held in Seattle and our mission felt that this course was important for all the missionaries to attend so they arranged for us to attend this session. One of the mission couples who were on furlough came and substituted for us in the dorm and our other duties for the week that we were absent. We needed the break and the knowledge that we gained from the course was good. Chuck realized, after attending the seminar, that he had bitterness in his heart toward his father. When Chuck asked his father's forgiveness, Chuck then felt a new freedom spiritually and emotionally. We both realized that this course would be a benefit to the students in understanding their bitterness toward others (for the next several years all the students were taken to the spring seminars.)

Stoney Nicklie and Sarah Antoine could be seen chatting together more and more frequently. It was very evident that spring was here and the bloom of love shone in their eyes. Each evening Stoney took the garbage down to

---

10. John W. Peterson, Favorites (Number Seven) Singspiration, Inc. (Grand Rapids, 1971) p. 2

the pig stye to feed the pigs. Sarah felt that she needed to go along to help and the two of them were kidded about their trips to feed the pigs. Sarah shortly had an engagement ring and the two young people planned a June wedding.

Christian love was apparent between the students and staff. Bernie would come up to me and say 'Why doesn't my mother love me like you do?' It would tear my heart knowing that Bernie was taken away from her mother because she wasn't cared for. Bernie lived with her grandmother until she died and then was passed from foster home to foster home. Love was expressed in many ways. For example, when we hiked in the woods Mary walked before me and Bernie walked behind me to make sure that no tree or bush branches brushed against me as we passed.

Some of the girls in the dorm enjoyed doing beadwork in their free time. I received several necklaces and also bought some for Christmas gifts. Mary made Chuck a beautiful thunderbird bolo-tie.

Sorry to say, beadwork will shortly become a lost art, because many of the young women aren't interested in doing it.

Native people have an ingrained mistrust for white people. The Indian thinks that a white person's only interest in them is to get something from them. When they realize that a white person is there because of love and a desire to help the native people the barriers are broken down. An Indian can tell a phony immediately, but real love is returned with love.

Art Dick shared with us about his extreme hate for white people. Before becoming a Christian he had belonged to Red Power, an organization that planned the overthrow of government and white people through force. Art also said that the first time he experienced love for white people was while attending the Native Institute of Canada.

Chuck and I found fishing a relaxing sport. Neither of us had ever done any before coming to Canada. All of the lakes and streams around us had rainbow trout.

In the spring, at the very spot where we took our baths the first year, fishing was good. The pan-fried fish were small but were eaten many nights and enjoyed.

Some summer days just to sit with a pole in our hand at the quiet spot would relieve tension and provide supper.

The month of June, the last month of the Native Institute of Canada's first school year proved exceedingly busy. Some events were planned, some planned events were changed and some unexpected events took place. The month truly proved an expression we often heard at Boot Camp training, 'A missionary should always expect the unexpected.'

The Native Institute of Canada had one graduating student, Lewis Holmes, who received his high school diploma. The weekend after this graduation was Stoney and Sarah's wedding. Sarah had legal papers to process long before the wedding took place because Stoney wanted her to be legally declared a Protestant before they were married.

On Sarah's reserve all babies born were registered by the government as Catholic and when that person died they would be buried by a priest with a Catholic ceremony. The family had no say in the choice of ceremony. It could not be changed unless the individual went through a long drawn out legal process.

Since Sarah was now of an Evangelical faith Stoney wanted her to be legally declared so before they became husband and wife. The ceremony took place on Sarah's reserve, a six hour drive from the Native Institute of Canada.

Chuck, Charles, David and I went to our first native wedding (most of the native people we had met on the reserves lived common-law). The service was scheduled to begin at two but the bride and her uncle, who gave her away, did not arrive until three. The hall was decorated nicely and our daughter (which we called all our dorm girls) looked lovely in her white wedding dress. The reason Sarah's uncle gave her away was because her father was no longer living (her mother deserted her when she was small).

In Canada the wedding ceremony itself takes longer than one in the states because legal papers are filled out as part of the ceremony. This is done before the pastor pronounces the couple man and wife. The missionary who had led Sarah to the Lord performed the marrying while the missionary that she lived with and Gene Parkins also had a part in the ceremony. About an hour after the wedding was over the reception began. It too, was held in the hall; punch and cake were served. During the reception one after another of the Indian men and the missionaries (who had a part in the wedding) gave speeches. This was followed with the presents being opened by Sarah and Stoney. I believe the length of time from when we arrived at the lovely wedding to the end of the gift opening was about six hours, a record for the Temple family.

The next event in our calendar was Charles' graduation from the Quesnel High School. Two weeks after Charles' graduation was over, Pauline and Denny's wedding was scheduled in Seattle. During the two weeks Charles went on a ten day canoe trip, with his classmates, around the famous Bowren Lake Chain. David and one of his school friends visited his friend's grandparents outside of Vancouver on the beautiful coast of British Columbia for the two weeks. David planned to hitch-hike from Vancouver to Seattle.

Larry and Ellen were expecting an addition to their family. Larry made arrangements with Gene Parkins to borrow his car when it was time to take Ellen to the hospital.

On a Saturday morning close to the baby's due date Larry strolled over to our house and chatted with us for about a half hour. Then he nonchalantly said 'Ellen's contractions are coming about every five minutes.' We excitedly said almost in unison 'Larry, you should go borrow the car from Gene and take Ellen to the hospital right away.'

Larry strolled down to the Parkins' and repeated the same process; a half hour of conversation and then the bombshell 'Ellen is having contractions every five minutes.' Gene and Helen excitedly loaned their car. Larry calmly drove Ellen into the hospital, then when he learned that it would be a little while before the baby's arrival he went down to the hospital corridor to visit. Again Larry calmly chatted before breaking the news that he was to become a father any minute.

The whole situation was so typically Indian and Larry was probably having a good chuckle to himself every time he made his announcement and watched the white man get excited.

Helen and I took turns watching little Lucy while Ellen and the new baby were in the hospital. Classes were over and we could give active Lucy our undivided attention.

One afternoon Lucy and I were on the deck outside of our living room. Lucy was playing with her toys and I ran inside to put the meat in the oven for dinner. When I came back outside Lucy had disappeared.

Chuck and I started searching for her. We went from one end of the property to the other calling her name but did not find her. The fearful thought came to mind that she had gone into the woods and that we would never find her. We thought of bears, coyotes and wolves. Each septic tank hole was inspected in case she had fallen in. Chuck and I arrived at the Native Institute of Canada's gate just as the school bus arrived from town.

The two Parkins' girls stepped off the bus and to our surprise little Lucy was with them. Lucy had gotten about a half mile toward town when the two girls on the bus saw her. The bus driver stopped and asked Lucy what she was doing out on the road. Her response was 'going to town to see my mother.'

Chuck and I were so relieved to see Lucy that we didn't even scold her. As a matter of fact we were non-plussed at such daring determination in a three year old.

There were times during the first two years when I would be the only person on campus for 24 hours. The experience was not one I wanted or enjoyed doing but one I agreed to do because after accepting Christ I chose for my life verse, 'I can do all things through Christ who strengthens me.'

Many a time through life, I felt incapable of playing the piano for a meeting, or singing before any audience, or meeting people, or teaching Sunday School and then my life verse would come to mind. I would ask the Lord for His strength and then proceed to do whatever I was asked to do.

Solitude was a state enjoyable to me but absolute a-loneness was a new experience. My over active imagination thought about what I couldn't do against fire or even a man coming on campus with evil intentions. I feared pushing the wrong switch on the light plant before daylight or meeting a bear or wolf at night when turning the light plant off. Under a marvelously brilliant star studded sky I'd sing loudly all the way home from the light plant. The Lord was teaching me utter dependence upon Him.

The mission suggested that we go on deputation for the months of July and August. We prepared to leave from Pauline and Denny's wedding to contact churches and prayer partners all across the states.

But I am getting ahead of my story. At the Native Institute of Canada the plans for the summer building program was for the construction of a log A-frame school building (the dimensions of which were to be sixty feet wide and a hundred and twenty feet long); two cabins for married students and to refurbish the old school building into another staff home. The logs had already been cut in May and peeled with the help of church men who came up from the states.

Right after Stoney and Sarah's wedding Chuck drove the mission truck down to Vancouver to get a load of particle board for the A-frame flooring. After having the truck loaded he had driven just a few streets from the lumber company and started up a hill when the whole load of particle board slid off the back of the truck. Chuck had to pick up the heavy four by eight sheets himself to reload the truck until a 'good samaritan' came along and helped him. Then Chuck drove the truck back to the lumber company and had them bind the flooring so that it would not slide off again. A stop had to be made at the truck weighing station outside of Vancouver. They found that one of the axles was overweight. Chuck dejectedly sat down by the truck contemplating unloading and moving the boards when the official looked at him and said 'oh, go ahead'. An exhausted husband arrived home at three a.m.

The A-frame had the foundations in and the floor was ready to be laid by the time Charles and David left for their trips.

A church youth group from Bellingham, Washington were helping. This group had been up the summer before and Chuck and I had become close friends with one of the sponsors, Dick and Doris Cox. Sunday morning arrived and we had the morning service on the deck of the A-frame of which the hundred and twenty feet had just finished being nailed down the day before. (Chuck said when the men started nailing at one end they thought they would never reach the other end.) It was a beautiful clear morning and sitting in the open air, surrounded by trees and facing a lush meadow, to worship God was a blessed experience. That evening the service again was held on the deck. Chuck was leading the singing. When he asked for requests Dick asked to sing 'When the roll is called up yonder I'll be there'. Little did we know that in less than twenty-four hours this would be true for Dick. At lunch the next day Dick, seventy-two years of age, had a heart attack.

As soon as Doris realized that Dick wasn't feeling well she came in to get us and by the time we ran out to Dick he was already home with the Lord. Heart resuscitation was used and a helicopter was summoned from town to take Dick to the hospital, but we knew that Dick was already gone. When Chuck stepped over to console Doris and to tell her that Dick was home with the Lord, Doris said 'Oh, I'm so glad that Dick knew the Lord; you know he didn't accept the Lord until he was in his fifties.'

Another family who was helping had their little daughter with them. The little girl asked her mother 'What happened to Mr. Cox' and her mother responded, 'He has gone to heaven to be with Jesus.' After this family returned home to Minnesota a helicopter flew over one day and the mother heard her little girl whisper, 'I wonder who has gone to be with Jesus now.'

The funeral director made the arrangements for Dick's body to be taken down to Bellingham but someone was needed to drive Doris and her car and trailer down. We volunteered and quickly packed. Our car was left at the Native Institute of Canada so that Charles would have transportation to Seattle when he returned from the canoe trip.

Chuck and I arrived early from Bellingham, but that gave us a few extra days to prepare for the wedding. Charles and David both were to be ushers: Patti (who came up from California with her family), also was in the wedding party. Charles arrived with the car but David did not show up the day he said he would, or the next day, or the next day. We were worried (I'm sure I got quite a few more grey hairs. Chuck was already white) and had a prayer chain going. David had left his friend's grandmother's the day he had expected to; we found out this information when we called David's friend in Quesnel. Then we worried that something had happened to him while hitchhiking but this proved to not be the case.

David had with him Pauline's phone number of the apartment where she lived and we were all over to the new apartment getting it ready for occupancy. David did not know either address and every time he called the old apartment there was no answer. He too, was getting desperate since he had arrived the day he said he would in Seattle and when he couldn't locate us he went to stay with a friend (from the time we had lived in Seattle). We all did finally get together in time for the dress rehearsal.

The lovely wedding and reception went well. I couldn't help but think of the culture contrast - white culture wedding two hours; Indian culture wedding six hours. We were able to see our grandson and visit with Jim and Patti. My mother and father came up from California for the occasion. This was the last time I saw my father alive. He went home to be with the Lord in July, just a few days before his eighty-first birthday (while we were on deputation in Pennsylvania) in the same manner and at the same time of day as our friend Dick Cox.

# Chapter VII

Our car had thousands of miles added to its odometer during July and August. We visited family, friends, prayer partners and churches from Washington state to New Jersey to tell them about the things the Lord was doing among the native people in British Columbia.

We planned a trip to The King's College (my alma mater) while we were east. Charles had filled out applications to several Christian colleges, including King's for fall entrance but he had not heard if he was accepted before he left home. As we were travelling, Charles had been praying that if the Lord wanted him to attend the King's College not only would he be accepted but that they would also have summer employment available for him.

We only remained on campus overnight. Charles was accepted and a summer job was open for him to start working the next morning. Now there were just three of us to travel the rest of the trip.

The reason that the mission felt it was necessary for us to go out on a summer deputation was because our income averaged about four hundred and fifty dollars a month. This was too low an amount to effectively minister. Still it was not the Lord's timing to increase our support. We left the Native Institute of Canada with a tankful of gas and ten dollars in our pocket. Two months later we returned with a tankful of gas and fifteen dollars in our pocket. During the entire trip each love gift we received was just the correct amount of money to get us to the next destination; it covered car expenses, food and lodging. When we returned at the end of August, we had promised twenty additional dollars per month. But through succeeding years many of the people and churches that were contacted that summer were led by the Lord to financially support us.

Beside a suggested figure for monthly support the mission also had a housing requirement. For a family the sum was twenty-five hundred dollars. This money assured mission housing for each family as long as they stayed with the mission. We had planned on using a portion of the money from the sale of our house in Seattle to pay the twenty-five hundred dollars. But the Lord did not sell our house until nineteen seventy-six. Instead he arranged for this payment through the dear people in Landgren Church. How thrilled we were when we learned this. Also before the end of this year Landgren Church pledged to us half our needed monthly support.

A few years after this trip the Lord saw fit to supply most of our financial needs through the usual channel of gifts being sent to the home office and the mission issuing us a support check. About once or twice a year we would be reminded of His complete capability of caring for our financial needs by sending us a low support check and then He would meet our needs through other channels.

We brought my mother home to visit when we returned from our deputation trip. For the next eight years, until she went home to be with the Lord, she would visit six weeks to three months each year. Mother always remarked about the blessing she received from being on the mission field with us. She would sometimes say 'If I had my life to live over I would have a log house to live in.' My mother not only enjoyed the surroundings but she loved the native young people and they loved her. All the students called her grandma.

Life expectancy is much lower in the Indian culture than the white culture, due to a high mortality rate and suicide. If the native lived past sixty years of age they were greatly respected. A person living to eighty years of age (like mother) was very unusual and considered very wise. Many students would come to mother just to hear her talk.

Mother was a big help to me. She enjoyed handiwork and my mending was always taken care of while she visited. She took pleasure in doing my ironing and a pile of unironed clothes would be waiting for her each time she visited. Many other little jobs that lady missionaries never seem to have time to get done can be done by grand-moms. But the greatest thing that Mother did was the love that she showed. This example before people who have never experienced living in Christian homes is invaluable.

The A-frame was ready for use; new staff members and new students, as well as most of the former students were assembled for fall classes.

Our new school building's main floor housed a large gymnasium; next to which was the dining hall (used also for meetings and services), the kitchen and one classroom. The second floor contained two classrooms, the library and three offices. For a few years the basement remained unfinished.

The first winter a huge barrel stove was constructed that took six foot long logs and it was installed in the basement. We were never very warm in the A-frame that winter. The gym never had been insulated. When the sub-zero temperatures came, the young people would play volley-ball, basketball and floor hockey in their winter clothing. This place for sports was much used and greatly appreciated.

Now the house next to the A-frame was the Parkins home. (On the other side of the A-frame was the old trapper's cabin where we lived the first year. It was not used this school year.) Next to the Parkins' house was the building where Stoney and the male students previously lived. The interior had been changed into a one bedroom apartment for Stoney and Sarah with a dorm of three bedrooms in the back.

A new married students cabin had been placed between the second and third building. Three young women were assigned to this house. Two of the women were students from Arctic Bible Institute in Alaska who were down to the Native Institute of Canada for their internship year. Roberta Neeley, an Indian, was scheduled to do the cooking for the students and Esther helped in the school office doing secretarial work. The third woman, Marjorie Beardmore from Vancouver, was a new teacher for the high school.

The next building, the old school house, was now converted into a staff home for Bob and Deloris Eldridge, their two daughters and Deloris' two sisters. Bob came to the Native Institute of Canada to be the maintenance man and Deloris helped in many areas including secretarial work, campus hostess and chairman for social activities.

The next building was our house and the dormitory. Beside which was Larry, Ellen and Lucy's cabin. After Larry and Ellen's cabin was the other new married couple's cabin, the last building on campus. It housed a young man Doug Stone, who came to help with maintenance, and three male students.

Art and Sharon Dick were the only former students who did not return to school. Lewis came for first year Bible School subjects and the rest of the students continued in courses that followed those of the previous year.

The girls dorm was filled but within a month's time some of the girls returned home because of homesickness, leaving six girls. More and more boys kept arriving and the staff decided to switch dorms. The six girls went to live in the three dorm rooms at Stoney and Sarah's. We ended up with fourteen boys to counsel and to be a mother and dad to. Ten slept in our five dorm rooms and three were over in the cabin with Doug.

Many of the new high school and Bible School students were from the Blackfoot tribe in Alberta, about eight hundred miles from the Native Institute of Canada. They had interesting last names like Back Fat, Raw Eater, Fox and Yellow Old Woman.

Vincent Yellow Old Woman, the young man who had helped on campus the summer of nineteen seventy-one was now here for Bible School classes. Although that had been his intention the previous summer, he never followed through and left for home before classes started. Vincent was not able to stand at home and constantly succumbed to drink.

One night he returned home from a drinking spree with his buddies and later that night realized that his best friend's house was on fire. Vincent tried to rescue his friend, who was in a drunken stupor on his bed, but could not get into the bedroom because of the flames and heat. When Vincent saw this young man die, he thought, 'There but for the grace of God go I'. From that time on Vincent was able to stand. After his year at the Native Institute of Canada he went to another Bible School and eventually became a pastor to his own people.

Two Eskimo boys, Paul Pemik and James Karetak from Eskimo Point, Northwest territories were students this year.

Their village missionary had sent them to a Bible School down in the states but when the two young men arrived at the border, the customs officials would not let them into the states. After the missionary received a phone call from the border he contacted other missionaries and learned of the Native Institute of Canada's existence. The boys were called and told to travel up to Quesnel where they enrolled in the first year Bible School classes.

One morning at breakfast we heard a loud SQUEEK-EEK and then silence. Everyone looked at everyone and then all went searching the house to see if we could find what caused the squeek-eek. Nothing could be found.

That evening when I went to the refrigerator to prepare dinner I noticed that the food in the freezer part was defrosting. Immediately I thought, what are we going to do now? We are so far from town any repairs would be sky high. Also I thought that we couldn't afford a new refrigerator if it couldn't be fixed. It would be a back breaking job to haul the huge double door refrigerator freezer to town.

The next morning Chuck took off the back panel of the refrigerator and there in the fan was the remains of a mouse caught in the fan. The loud squeek-eek was its final cry as it jammed itself into the blade. Chuck removed the tiny creature, the fan started and all went well with the refrigerator. My fears and concerns about repairs had been for nothing, as often happens in a Christian's life.

Many little furry creatures decided that all the new buildings that had been built in their meadow, would make a good lodging place for them in the cold weather. The school staff kept busy setting mouse traps. That is, everyone except us. We depended upon our cat, Topper, to keep the furry creatures away. She did a good job, except for the one that got into the refrigerator.

The Parkins' decided that it would be a good idea to borrow Topper since their traps were being ignored. Of course, being a typical cat, when Topper was placed in the

Parkins' house she just slinked around with the strangeness of the different home and hid herself under a piece of furniture. Helen, who didn't like cats in the first place, decided that a cat was useless for mouse catching and Topper was quickly returned to our house.

For our Sunday evening service sometimes the chairs would be placed in a circle. We were sitting in this manner when I looked across the room and there was a little mouse running around the chair legs and in between student's feet. Everyone was singing choruses and oblivious to the play beneath their feet.

I pondered, 'Should I keep quiet, or should I say something so they can lift their feet? How much confusion would it cause?' I finally decided that I should say something when I noticed that Gene was aware of the circumstances and looking at me. He shook his head 'no'. So I kept quiet and watched the mouse play. My name would have been mud with the girls if they had known that I let a mouse play between their feet and never said a word.

Chuck's schedule was slightly more crowded than before. He now took care of the bookkeeping along with his other duties. Daily Chuck would make entries and write checks but once a month when it was time to balance the books, long hours were spent in finding some small error. Chuck had never done any bookkeeping before and he learned what to do and what not to do as he did it.

Marjorie Stone took over the teaching of science. Now Chuck was free to teach some Bible School subjects. He taught Doctrine the first semester and the second semester taught both Doctrine and Romans.

Then late in the second semester Chuck was asked to become Dean of Students and more counselling was added to the already busy schedule. All the staff members counsselled students from time to time but now any discipline problems went to Chuck.

I had enjoyed cooking for the students but was very happy that the school now has a cook. In order for the cook to have a few days off each week the staff took turns cooking on the weekends. Our turn came every five weeks. The staff also ate some meals with the students.

One staff family would eat lunch and dinner for one week in the dining hall on a rotating basis. This helped to develop a good rapport with the students. Possible discipline problems were also more easily prevented with the staff being in the dining room.

This year Ellen prepared Larry and Lucy's meals in their own cabin. (A policy which continued for married couples through the years.)

My food preparation was now for Chuck and David, except of course for the times that I cooked or we ate in the A-frame. It seemed peculiar to be making such small quantities of food.

The French class that I taught was now held up in the new school classroom but music classes, music lessons and choir practice was still held in my home because a piano was there. A piano was not purchased for the A-frame until another year had passed.

One project the men were working on in between classes was the completion of the sewer system. Gene and Chuck picked up a cement lid for a septic tank and Chuck injured his back. The pain in his back was terrible and in a few days the pain spread to his hip and a short time later the pain travelled on down his leg.

Chuck went to a chiropractor in Quesnel but relief after a treatment was very short. After three treatments the chiropractor told Chuck that he should go to see a medical doctor. All fall the doctor told Chuck to rest in bed and take the prescribed muscle relaxer and pain killer. Chuck would stay in bed a few days or a week, then he would get up and do all his work as usual but he was never free from pain.

Students and staff were attending Wednesday night prayer meeting in the A-frame when the lights went out all over the campus. A glow could be seen out the window in the direction of the light plant building. The men rushed out and when they got to the fire they realized that nothing could be done to save the light plant or the building. Their next concern was about the containers of gasoline close by. Two fifty gallon drums blew but there was also a three hundred gallon tank right next to the burning building. The men formed a bucket brigade to the creek and threw a blanket over the drum. Chuck climbed on top of the blanket and poured the water from each bucket handed to him down onto the blanket. The tank was saved!

When we arrived back at our apartment both of the kerosene lamps were empty so David took them outside to fill. After I lit them the flame travelled down the wick and was dancing all over the top of the fluid. David had put the fluid from the gasoline container into the lamps instead of from the kerosene container. Both containers were unmarked and the contents could only be detected by smelling. David thought only kerosene was kept in the unmarked container.

I quickly picked both lamps up, ran to the kitchen and poured the burning liquid down the drain. Only by God's grace was a second fire averted that night.

We didn't have electricity that night and we also didn't have water because the electric pump was run by the light plant. The next day a small light plant that had been kept for a spare, was hooked up. Each building had to take turns hooking up appliances. Certain homes could run their refrigerator certain hours and then unplug them so other homes could run theirs.

Patti and our eighteen month old grandson were able to visit with us for a week. They had a flight from Witchita, Kansas to Vancouver to Quesnel. Patti will never forget the flight; airsickness and fog so bad the plane could not land in Quesnel.

The airline provided all Quesnel travellers with taxi rides for the last seventy-five miles of their journey at night through 'pea soup' thick fog.

When Patti and Patrick arrived three hours late the luggage with some of the baby's clothes did not accompany them (the airline located it six months later).

At this age, Patick could say quite a few words but whether he knew the words or not he loved to talk and would jabber if he couldn't think of any words to say.

The Indian young people couldn't get over Patrick's boldness and they were almost afraid of his constant talking. Native children are taught to be shy and quiet.

A new neighbor who had moved to the Baker Creek community recently, heard about the light plant being destroyed by fire. The man worked for the phone company and told us about a spare light plant that his company had. The school was able to purchase it. It was a larger size and had better efficiency than the light plant that burned. We never questioned God's wisdom in allowing the old light plant to burn because we saw how much better the new light plant that He planned for us to have fit the needs of the campus of the Native Institute of Canada.

Clothes fashions always seemed to arrive in Quesnel about five years after they were in style down south.

One such fashion was the year of the mini-skirt. How ridiculous it looked for women to wear a mini-skirt with temperatures at fifty-five below zero. But they were sure they were stylish.

It's a wonder all the young women didn't get frost-bitten legs.

Native Conferences were held for the first time this year. In November and April village missionaries would bring car loads of people from the reserves to the Native Institute of Canada for three days. A native pastor or Bible teacher was brought to speak and native singers shared in song. We averaged between one hundred and a hundred and fifty Indian people in attendance both fall and spring conference each this year.

All the students slept on the floor of their dorm parent's living room and the guests were housed in the dorm rooms. When all the dorm rooms were filled the classroom floors were used (mattresses were put down for comfort). Each person brought their own bed roll. We used to joke and say that at conference time we had wall to wall people.

Native Christians were blessed through the conference ministry and many unbelievers were led to the Lord. Often a Christian Indian would be the only person on the reserve who knew the Lord. They would feel very alone and often rejected by other reserve members. They had no fellowship at home but attending conference gave them fellowship and strength as they saw and spoke with fellow Christians.

Native speakers relate to the Indian culture in a more meaningful way than any white person could. The guests received a blessing in the messages and music.

Before I had cooked for sixteen to twenty people now I had to prepare food for a hundred and fifty. Each staff family prepared two meals at Conference time. We had large quantity cook books and usually had no problems in preparing enough food. But one Conference when it was my turn to cook breakfast the menu listed 'cream of wheat'. My family had never cared for cream of wheat so I had never cooked it! There was no recipe for it in the large quantity cookbook. I asked the other missionary wives if they made cream of wheat for breakfast and one gave me a recipe that served four people.

At six a.m. my multiplication didn't work too well and when it came time to serve breakfast the cream of wheat looked like a big pot of cement. A line up of people approached the serving counter and each person's facial expression showed surprise as they watched Chuck attempt to pry a ball of thick, thick, thick cream of wheat off of a serving spoon into a bowl. We had lots left over and it was put in the freezer. About six mornings later a chunk of the frozen gruel was cut off and dropped into a large pot of water. It came out the right consistency that morning.

An announcement came in the mail that the Prince George Choral Society was going to give a performance of the Messiah early in December. I thought that if we took the students to hear this great work it would be a good learning experience for them. Early in October I started the study of this Oratorio. Each student had a different project to write on the life of George Frederick Handel. The man's life and works were discussed in class. The Bible texts that were set to the music of 'The Messiah' were studied and then the different passages were listened to on records. The students eagerly studied and enjoyed the projects and classroom work. They grew to appreciate the music; were blessed by the words and looked forward to a live performance.

All staff vehicles were packed with students and their lunch bags, the day we went north to Prince George. It was a very cold morning with much snow and ice on the road. Our car took the lead with David at the steering wheel because driving irritated Chuck's back. About half-way to our destination there was a turn in the road but due to the ice the wheels of our car did not turn and we found ourselves in a ditch piled with snow. When we looked out the car window the road was above the top of our car and we could see the wheels of other cars passing.

Everyone in our car checked everyone else and we were all unharmed. Gerald Tom was in the back seat and he said he thought 'Here I go again!'

We saw that there was no way to get the car out of the ditch except by tow truck. Neither Chuck nor I had any extra money with us nor a check book to pay for a tow truck. David said he would hitch hike back to Quesnel, get a blank check from a friend's mother and arrange for a tow truck to get the car out of the ditch. While we were waiting for David to return the other cars in our caravan came along, spotted us and stopped. The students and I squeezed into the other cars and went on ahead.

David wasn't long getting to town and back. The tow truck had no difficulty getting the car out of the ditch so Chuck and David still arrived before the performance of the Messiah began.

We could not all get seats together. As the Oratorio progressed I realized that there was one thing of which I had forgotten to inform the students. Between each selection I heard a spattering of clapping coming from here and there over the auditorium and I knew it came from the members of my class. I had told them to stand for the Hallelujah Chorus but I had not told them to refrain from clapping. After a while the clapping was no longer heard because an usher had informed them that applause was not customary.

We arrived home late that night but both students and staff felt that the time spent in travel and listening had been well worthwhile. As I was dozing off to sleep I woke with a start. I just came to the realization that the check I had filled out to pay for the tow truck was not drawn on the bank in which we had an account. I had been so careful to put our account number on David's friend's mother's check but the bank name had not registered until sleep time. David went to the towing company the next day and paid them in cash for the service. They returned the check and the fear of the Quesnel paper headlines of 'Missionary Defrauds Towing Company' was averted.

We usually get our Christmas tree from the woods early in December each year so that the students could enjoy it before going home for a Christmas break. Usually a couple of the boys would join in the trimming of the tree. It was great fun for them since they never had a tree in their homes.

A week after the performance of 'The Messiah' I gave a Christmas concert in Quesnel. The idea of giving a concert had come from a missionary conference that Chuck and I had attended in October. The speaker had concentrated his messages on going a second and third mile in mission giving.

A friend of mine who is a pastor's wife told me how she had little extra money for missions and that the Lord had led her to hold an art show with her paintings. The money she received from the sale of her pictures she gave to missions. So the idea of a concert came to my mind for second mile giving in my life.

The Quesnel weekly newspaper 'The Cariboo Observer' advertised the concert twice.

Thursday, December 7, 1972 the paper stated

Two women from the Native Institute of Canada at Nazko will give a recital December 16, at 2 p.m. in the music room at Correlieu Senior Secondary School.

Soprano June Temple and violinist Helen Parkins will present **Christmas Around the World,** including selections from the Messiah, the famous oratorio by Handel. A collection will be taken for the Institute.

The Institute is a dormitory school providing academic, technical and commercial training, and basic training for skill development. It is especially geared to older Indian students who wish to finish high school. (there was no mention of the Bible School.)

Thursday, December 14, 1972 the following appeared:

TO ALL
MUSIC LOVERS
A SPECIAL CHRISTMAS RECITAL
featuring
MRS. JUNE TEMPLE - SOPRANO
MRS. HELEN PARKINS - VIOLINIST
will be held at the
CORRELIEU SENIOR SECONDARY SCHOOL
Music Room
SUNDAY, DECEMBER 16, 2 P.M.

On the day of the recital the following Christmas selections were performed. Although the songs selected represented many countries the words were all sung in English.

1.  Helen Parkins - Violin
    Hark! The Herald Angels Sing..Mendelssohn-Barthoedy
    O Little Town of Bethlehem..Redner
    Silent Night..Gruber

2.  June Temple - Voice
    I wander as I wonder..Niles Horton
    A Chinese Christmas Carol..T'ien-hsiang
    Manger Lullaby..Newton
    Angels from Heaven..Guenther
    Sweet Little Jesus Boy..Spiritual

3.  Helen Parkins - Violin   June Temple - Voice
    Jesu Bambino..Pietro A Yon

4.  June Temple - Voice
    The Birthday of A King..Neidlinger

5.  Helen Parkins - Violin
    O Holy Night..Adam

6.  June Temple - Voice
    Christmas..McEnaney

108

7.  June Temple · Voice  Helen Parkins · Violin
    Selections from the Messiah..George Frederick Handel
    There were shepherds abiding in the field
    And Lo, the Angel of the Lord Came Upon Them
    And the Angel said unto them
    Come unto Him
Recital Pianist..Phyllis Epp


Some of the students were having difficulty paying for their room and board. (There were no tuition fees for the students). The collection received from the recital went toward the meeting of these expenses. Although it wasn't a large amount of money, I felt that the hours spent in practice were worthwhile.

Just a few days after my concert the doctor put Chuck in the hospital because of his increasing back pain. He was released just a few days before Christmas.

We had all planned on going to Pauline's and Denny's for the holiday. For a while we thought our plans needed changing with Chuck in the hospital however that was not necessary.

Charles flew home from college and the four of us plus Mary Angus drove down to Seattle. We only had two days before the holiday to get the shopping done. It was good having Mary share the holiday with us. My mother flew up from California to join us in the festivities.

Before it was time to leave for home, Chuck had to be flown up to Vancouver for emergency surgery (it had nothing to do with his back injury). The boys, Mary and I drove up to Vancouver and had a revolting discovery at the border when we learned that we had to pay duty on our Christmas gifts. After visiting with Chuck a couple days in the hospital we saw that his recovery was progressing nicely so we drove on home. Chuck flew home a week later. **His recuperation** progressed well but he had a great deal of pain, due to a complication that developed in the hospital the day after his surgery.

It took about a month for Chuck to gain his strength and be free of pain. One night when he was very uncomfortable one of our boys, Jonathon Raw Eater, had a dispute and started hitch hiking for home. When Chuck heard about this he and Gene Parkins went after Jonathon to counsel him. The boy had gotten about forty miles from the Native Institute of Canada before the men found him. Jonathon returned but Chuck spent a night of great discomfort because of his giving of himself to bring Jonathon home.

One of the treatments to help Chuck recuperate was for him to submerge three times a day in a tub of water as hot as he could stand. Since the hot water was not yet hooked up to our tub I had to attach a hose to the tub in the dormitory wash room, run the hose through the halls to our tub, go back to the dormitory wash room and start the water running. Then pray I wouldn't forget the water was running while I did other things until the tub was full.

Gerald Tom was also very sick with the flu during Chuck's recuperation time. Gerald needed care and I was constantly travelling from one bedroom to the other many times each day. I was getting plenty of nursing experience even though the Lord had shut the door on my being a missionary nurse when I was young. The past two years and for one more year I had to make many decisions concerning the student's health care. A full time nurse then came on staff and I was relieved of this responsibility for which I felt very inadequate.

While Chuck was in the Vancouver hospital the Lord made a very interesting church contact. A family at Landgren church had at one time lived outside of Vancouver and attended a Baptist church in Richmond, British Columbia. This family contacted Pastor Strauss, of the Richmond church, and told him about Chuck being in the hospital. How surprised Chuck was, being in a city where he knew no one, to have a pastor come call on him. From that time on Pastor Strauss and his congregation have shown a great love and interest toward our family and ministry.

Water was scarce at the Native Institute of Canada. Except for Chuck's sits-bath, water was rationed. Everyone was allowed only one bath or shower a week and even this was measured. The tub had a tape line, above which the water was not to exceed, giving each person about two inches of water. For the shower in the dorm, the individual was supposed to turn the water on to get wet; turn the water off while soaping up and again turn the water on to rinse.

The wells were just not sufficient for the number of people living at the Native Institute of Canada. After the winter was ended the pump was taken out of the well and put in the creek. Now there was plenty of water but it was yellow in color. (Some guests thought they were drinking lemonade.)

The Eldridge's had taken over the outreach to the community youth that Chuck and I had begun several years before. Bob and Deloris organized a Sunday evening youth fellowship with the Native Institute of Canada students and the community youth combined. Several of the neighboring young people accepted the Lord through this ministry. Social events were also planned for the combined group.

One such social was a mile long banana split. Bob went to town and purchased a thirty foot rain gutter. This was filled with bananas, ice cream and toppings. The young people lined up on both sides of the pipe. They were shoulder to shoulder with spoons in their hands. All had a great time once the word 'go' was given.

Another social event was a Valentine's banquet. Each boy was supposed to invite a girl to attend the banquet with him.

In preparation for the big event Chuck and I had an evening of practice with our fourteen boys. A dinner date is not common practice in Indian or Eskimo culture.

We explained how each boy was to go and knock on Stoney and Sarah's door. Then wait in the living room for the girl to come join him and together walk to the A-frame where the banquet was being held. Chuck explained and I practiced with each fellow the procedure of their offering their arm and my putting my arm through theirs to walk and how to slide a dining room chair under me as I sat at the table. The boys thought rehearsal was fun.

During this evening we asked the boys what was customary in their villages for dating or courting. They told us there was no such practice.

The Eskimo boys said that in their village when a young man was ready to live with a girl he would pick the one he wanted and go to her home. Then he would take her away. Either the girl would come willingly or he would drag her away. The girl's parents never protested.

One Indian fellow said that in his village the parents arranged a marriage and the young people had very little say in the choice of their partner.

In none of the student's cultures was there ever any physical contact in public before or after marriage.

Our own children had grown up seeing Chuck and me hug and kiss in our home. They accepted this as a natural expression of affection. But we refrained from doing this now knowing that it was an offense to the students. I missed this freedom of physically expressing my affection.

When Chuck and I went for a walk we did hold hands or I would hold his arm. The students would often say to us jokingly, 'no physical contact allowed' and Chuck would respond, 'Oh, we have a license allowing us to do this' and the students would laugh.

Doug Stone had declared when he arrived at the Native Institute of Canada that he was going to be a 'bachelor until the rapture' but after a few short months it became apparent that this was a misstatement. Doug and Marjorie Beardmore began to see more and more of each other and then they asked if they could use our apartment for their courting. The two of them would sit at our dining room table with a scrabble board in front of them. Every once in a while they would form a word on the board and the rest of the time they would stare into each other's eyes. Other nights Doug and Marjorie would sit on our sofa and chat softly. They were in such a world of their own that they never knew that Chuck and I were sitting in the living room. It was important that everytime the students saw Doug and Marjorie together that they would be in the presence of other staff members.

In an Indian village any time two people of the opposite sex were seen alone it was believed that they were together for immoral purposes. Doug and Marjorie wanted to prevent any such ideas or rumors from starting.

A party was given to announce Doug and Marjorie's

engagement. Staff and students joined in the festivities in the nicely decorated dining hall. When Doug gave Marjorie the ring and kissed her all the native fellows turned their heads away and the girls put their hands over their eyes. Even though the couple was now engaged they still had to make sure that they were only seen together in the company of other staff. (A June wedding was planned to occur right before the closing of the school. Marjorie had a lovely spot picked out in the meadow for the ceremony. Unfortunately, it snowed the day of the wedding and the service was held inside the A-frame.)

David was in his senior year at Quesnel high school. Shortly before the last semester was to begin David asked if it would be possible for him to finish his year in a Christian School. David was having a very difficult time standing for the Lord. There were no Christian young men his age in school and the friends he had there were involved with marijuana and drugs. David would try to resist the pressures and temptations; then give into them and be ashamed. His marks were also being affected. The cycle had continued for over a year and David wanted to break out of it.

Pauline was teaching in the same Christian High School in Seattle in which I taught previous to coming with the mission. After Chuck and I discussed the problem with Pauline, Denny and David, we all came to the conclusion that it would be best for David to stay with Pauline and Denny to finish his term at Seattle Christian School. We are so thankful for this 'way of escape' that the Lord supplied. David was able to stand and his marks became much improved.

Our youngest child had been gone only a few weeks when in the midst of all the students and busyness I began to develop a loneliness in my heart for my children. In a way I felt that the Lord had cheated me because He had allowed the other three children to be home through all twelve grades of school but not David. Little did I know that in later years the Lord would allow David to live at home longer than any of the other children. My complaint to the Lord was unfounded.

Then Satan brought to mind a statement that one of my daughters had said to me, two years before, in anger. The phrase was that she didn't ever want to live near me. I wondered why she felt that way, then I wondered what I had ever done to her to cause such an outburst. To me, one of the most pleasurable things was to be near my mother. Was I so very different in the way I had raised my daughter that she would feel that way toward me? In my closet the tears ran down my cheeks until one day I realized the words of a song I had been singing.

Oh! To be Like Thee

O! to be like Thee, blessed Redeemer,
This is my constant longing and prayer;
Gladly I'll forfeit all of earth's treasures,
Jesus, thy perfect likeness to wear.
O! to be like Thee, O! to be like Thee,
Blessed Redeemer, pure as Thou art;
Come in Thy sweetness, come in Thy fullness,
Stamp Thine own image deep on my heart.

O! to be like Thee, full of compassion,
Loving, forgiving, tender and kind,
Helping the helpless, cheering the fainting,
Seeking the wand'ring sinner to find.
O! to be like Thee, O! to be like Thee,
Blessed Redeemer, pure as Thou art;
Come in Thy sweetness, come in Thy fullness,
Stamp Thine own image deep on my heart.

O! to be like Thee, lowly in spirit.
Holy and harmless, patient and brave;
Meekly enduring cruel reproaches,
Willing to suffer, others to save.
O! to be like Thee, O! to be like Thee,
Blessed Redeemer, pure as Thou art;
Come in Thy sweetness, come in Thy fullness;
Stamp Thine own image deep on my heart.

O! to be like Thee, Lord, I am coming,
Now to receive th' anointing divine,

114

All that I am and have I am bringing,
Lord from this moment all shall be Thine.
O! to be like Thee, O! to be like Thee,
Blessed Redeemer, pure as Thou art;
Come in Thy sweetness, come in Thy fullness,
Stamp Thine own image deep on my heart.

O! to be like Thee, while I am pleading.
Pour out Thy Spirit, fill with Thy love,
Make me a temple meet for Thy dwelling,
Fit me for life and heaven above.
O! to be like Thee, O! to be like Thee,
Blessed Redeemer, pure as thou art;
Come in Thy sweetness, come in Thy fullness;
Stamp Thine own image deep on my heart.[11]

I had been singing that I wanted to be like Christ. Through being rejected I realized the total rejection that Christ had felt from His own family, friends, tribe and nation. How great was my Lord's love for me to willingly go through his rejection on earth and rejection from his Heavenly Father when He took my sin upon Himself in order for me to have eternal life. I realized that nothing I had experienced could compare to this. Satan's power was broken and I was free of the misery that I had gone through.

Indians have quite a sense of humor. They often played jokes on each other or else were saying something ridiculous with a very straight face.

One girl would often come out with a remark that always cracked me up. The remark would usually come from Naomi's lips whenever the young people would get boisterous. The remark was, 'Oh, don't be such a savage.' Somehow, to hear this coming from an Indian's lips never seemed appropriate, which made it especially funny.

One of the customs in the Northwest Territories is that the day after the ice left the lakes the young men took

---

11. Ralph Carmichal, Carl Seal, Dan Burges, Rev. Ray DeVries, Lillian Merrill, Bill Cole, Bruce Howe, Don Stover, Jarrill McCracken, The New Church Hymnal, Lexicon Music Inc. Copyright 1976 p. 172

a swim. Paul and James wanted to follow the practice in Baker Creek. Some of the Indian boys thought they would join in the fun. Chuck and I stood on the bank to watch the boys dive off the bridge and swim in the frigid swollen creek in about thirty feet of water. When they came out of the water, some looked blue, others were shaking but all insisted that they weren't cold. I was afraid that they might come down with pneumonia but not one even came down with a sniffle.

This school year I did not have the staff join with the students for choir rehearsals or performances. Harmonizing had become easier for the students. They still sang in unison but they could also sing two and three part harmony. Some songs the men sang the melody and the girls harmonized with an alto part. Other songs some girls sang melody, other girls sang alto and the men in unison, harmonized. Only a few had learned to read music so most of the teaching method was by rote learning of the songs.

The choir received more invitations to give Sunday evening concerts in churches than they had in the year before. All the young people enjoyed singing and giving their testimonies at the meetings. Chuck usually closed with a devotional. The ministry of the Native Institute of Canada was becoming better known in Quesnel, Prince George and Williams Lake churches and the Native young people were becoming more relaxed in the presence of white people.

For years the media had portrayed Indian people as stonefaced and unemotional. The Indian people have reinforced the portrayal. Whenever an Indian person meets a white person for the first time the Indian will control his facial expressions. If the Indian person feels that the white person can be trusted (as the Indian gets to know the white person better) the Indian will not be near as guarded.

Chuck and I have seen the students smile, giggle, laugh, shout for joy, look sad, cry and mourn. Some of these emotions were seen by white church members and as they began to realize that Indian people aren't without feelings some of the barriers of prejudice started to break down.

Beside the choir, groups of three or four students were trained to go out as gospel teams to reserves to witness to their own people. Each team would practice several songs with one team member accompanying on a guitar.

When the gospel team arrived on the reserve, they would visit door to door. The missionary who worked on the reserve planned a meeting and the people from the homes visited would come to hear the team sing and give their testimonies. Through the years this ministry saw Native people come to accept the Lord as Saviour.

We had guests visiting on Mother's day and offered them our bedroom for the night. Chuck and I pulled our sofa-bed out to sleep in the living room. As I put on my pajamas I realized that I had forgotten to get my bathrobe but did not want to disturb the people in our bedroom to get it. Furthermore, I didn't think I would really need it. Then I heard the thundering of fourteen young men's feet coming down the dorm hallway toward our living room. I froze and realized that I was trapped when all fourteen young men stood in front of me. They were embarrassed and I was embarrassed. Then every young man's eyes rivetted on my face to prevent further embarrassment. I was presented with a homemade Mother's Day card with all the boy's signatures on it. The card was in the shape of a big igloo drawn by one of the Eskimo boys. It is a keepsake that I have never destroyed.

After the presentation, the group of young men turned toward the hallway. Every eye snapped from my face to the opposite direction. I appreciated how they worked at not causing me discomfort because of my being so poorly clothed.

It is not necessary for a private school to meet teacher's accreditation in British Columbia but the staff of the Native Institute of Canada felt it would be to the school's credit to meet these qualifications.

I wrote to the Board of Education in Vancouver to learn what I needed to do to get a teaching certificate in British Columbia. They suggested that I should take a few more education courses.

In a way it is amusing how each time a teacher moves

to another province (or state) that the Board of Education in the new province thinks it is necessary for the teacher to take more courses. When we moved to Washington state, I had two degrees and a Pennsylvania teacher's certificate yet the state of Washington required several education courses before they would issue me one of their certificates.

Now, British Columbia was following the same pattern. What was really ironic was the fact that British Columbia's Board of Education only requires a three year normal school course for teachers who were born, raised and educated in their province.

The next step for me was to find out how I was going to take two more education courses when the nearest University was four hundred and fifty miles away. Then I learned that the University of Wyoming offered education courses for credit by correspondence and the British Columbia Board of Education was willing to accept these credits if I took double the amount required from the University of British Columbia.

June, July and part of August in nineteen hundred and seventy-three, I spent time daily studying 'Educational Tests and Measurements.' The first half of the course gave insights in how best to design tests, whether they be multiple choice answers or the composition type. Then the later weeks concentrated on different methods of marking a test. It was an interesting course but the second half required a lot of mathematics and graph work (which I had not done since high school) and took me a longer time to complete an assignments than the first half. Since the summer was not near as complicated as those of the years before it was a pleasure to study again.

Charles was home from college and David had graduated from Seattle Christian High School; so he was home also. Chuck and I were both able to attend David's graduation. Both boys now had jobs and were working in the mill in Quesnel.

There was a major exodus when the Native Institute of Canada's classes finished. Of course, the students went home. The Parkins went down to the states for a summer furlough. Roberta and Esther returned home to Alaska.

Doug and Marjorie returned to the states to go to Bible School following the honeymoon. The Eldridges transferred to Alaska and the Nicklies went on holiday. Only the Temples remained on campus.

But we were not alone for long. Dan and Ginger Work were able to return to help. Dan's back had improved enough that the doctor would now allow him to drive our bad road.

An unexpected experience came about from having taught French these last two years.

On July first, Canadians celebrate Dominion day, which is a similar holiday to that of the fourth of July in the United States; a celebration in honor of the birth of the country.

The Baker Creek Community had a special 'do' (as they called it) on the Saturday after July first, which was held at the hall. The day long celebration, planned by the Ladies Club, began at ten a.m. and continued on into the night. People from the Native Institute usually joined in the morning and afternoon activities.

I arrived at ten a.m., this year, in time for the flag raising ceremony. Being available, I was asked to lead the singing of the national anthem. Well, I had opened French class every morning with the singing of 'O, Canada' in French and did not know the English words. So I led the singing of the national anthem in French while everyone else in the community sang it in English.

(In another year French became elective instead of a required subject in British Columbia. Since no Native students elected to study the subject it was no longer taught at the Native Institute of Canada. But for years, every time I heard the national anthem, I thought of the words in French.)

There were all kinds of games and contests on this Baker Creek Day 'do'; children's games, a horseshoe throwing competition, a baseball game and a ping pong tournament. A trophy was given to the winning pair of the ping pong tournament and it would spend six months in one person's home and six months in the other person's home before going back to the tournament to be given again. One year Charles shared it, another year David and another year, Stoney.

This day always proved to be the major fund raising event for the Baker Creek Ladies Club. They sold candy, hot dogs and pop. Lots were consumed.

No major construction was planned for this summer. Instead, Chuck, Dan and the youth groups who came to help, concentrated on doing a lot of finishing work inside the buildings. Chuck was still in great pain which increased as the summer progressed.

Late in August, right before lunch a customs official arrived on campus. He wanted to look through the school's books, around the property and ask many questions concerning the gifts and materials that had been donated to the school from people and churches in the states.

After several hours the official saw that everything was legal and in order. Chuck invited him down to our home for a cup of coffee. Stoney and Sarah were back from holiday and visiting when the official arrived and Stoney whispered to Sarah, 'Don't say one word.' The two of them sat in absolute silence in fear that they would say something that they shouldn't to a government official.

The middle of August I started on the second course which was titled 'Community Resources for Continuing Education'. This course was more interesting than the first. Its purpose was to acquaint the teacher with all the historical, geographical and commercial information of the community in order to plan educational trips for students. I learned a great deal about Quesnel and the Baker Creek area which made me appreciate the community more than before. My British Columbia teachers certificate was issued after the course was completed.

With only a few staff men on campus and not too many youth groups to help out during the progression of the summer months, some things did not get done. One of those things was the cutting of the grass around the buildings.

I thought that it would be good exercise for me to push the lawnmower so I started to spend a couple of hours each afternoon doing just that.

One afternoon a metal hanger was hidden in high grass. As I passed over it, it wrapped around the blade of the mower. I knew better but thought, oh, I can pull this out easily. So I pulled the hanger but it did not budge. Instead the metal gripped my hand and badly stung and bruised it from the blades spinning reverberation. Fortunately the Lord gave me the presence of mind to shut the motor off. I had a sore hand for several days but was thankful that nothing worse had happened to it.

A few families from Lewiston, Idaho came several summers to help out. This year one family decided to go camping way out in the bush after they ended their time at the school. The family was traveling in a camper, but it did not contain enough sleeping space inside for all the family. Therefore, Doug, the teenage son, slept outside on a cot.

After supper and a blazing campfire, the family settled into their warm sleeping bags for the night. Doug looked up at the spectacular star-studded sky for a while before closing his eyes. He had not gotten to sleep yet when he began to feel a very heavy pressure on his chest. When Doug opened his eyes, there was a black bear with it's forepaws on his chest looking past the cot toward the picnic table.

Doug knew that there was a possibility of a bear coming close, but he never expected one that close, especially since he was not too great a distance from the campfire. Because of the knowledge of the possibility of a bear, Doug had a gun within reach. He might need it to shoot over a bear's head to frighten it away or in case it was necessary to protect himself from a bear. The latter was true this time, and Doug lifted the gun and shot right into the bear's ear.

Everyone came running out of the camper asking what was wrong. They found a slumped bear with Doug underneath. To say that this would be a never forgotten trip for this family is absolutely true. They never felt the protection of the Lord more than at this time.

## Chapter VIII

In the fall ten of our boys returned to school and the dorm was full. Charles and David also went back to school. Charles returned to the Kings College and David started his studies at Prairie Bible Institute.

Just a few days after classes began, the doctor put Chuck in the Quesnel hospital. He was given a mylogram test which showed that back surgery was necessary. Since this was major surgery it was scheduled to be done in a Vancouver hospital and Chuck was flown down.

I drove our car down to be with Chuck. Since Mother was visiting us at this time she accompanied me on the trip. Pastor Strauss arranged for us to stay in the home of a dear family who were members of his church. They lived only twenty minutes from the hospital.

By the time mother and I arrived, Chuck had already had his surgery and he was doing fine. The doctor and nurses said that Chuck's recovery was unusual - we believe it was a miracle. He didn't even need to stay in the hospital the usual length of time but was released in nine days and flown home to Quesnel.

Our car had begun showing signs of much wear. On the trip down to Vancouver, it used many quarts of oil and had been doing so for several months. Chuck and I began to feel that when we went to a gas station we should say, 'Fill the oil and check the gas' instead of the other way around.

On the drive home from Vancouver the accelerator pedal became stuck in the full throttle position. As we zipped around the curves on the two lane highway through the Fraser Canyon, I tried to act as if this was natural driving for me, in order not to frighten my mother. For miles there was no shoulder to try to stop on and beyond the edge of the road was a sheer drop of many feet down to the river. Finally, I saw a gas station ahead and jerkingly applied the brakes as the engine zoomed at high speed. When I pulled off the road I turned the ignition off and we bucked to the gas pumps like a rodeo bucking horse entry. The expressions on both my mother's face and that of the gas attendants was one of total disbelief.

The gas pedal released with our unusual stopping and now that the oil and gas tanks were filled we had no more car problems for the rest of the journey. From this time on we started praying for a new vehicle.

Chuck was home, free of pain and feeling good. It had been just a little over a year since the ordeal had begun for him · a very difficult year. Beside the terrible pain Chuck also experienced great frustration in not being able to accompish the work he wanted to get done. Then there was spiritual depression also. He could not understand why the Lord was permitting him to go through this experience of not being able to function in the ministry as he thought he should.

The biggest problem of all for Chuck was his reaction to the large doses of Valium the doctor had prescribed. It wasn't until several years later that doctors started to limit the use of the drug because of the personality changes it brought about in the person taking it. Chuck's personality was unpleasantly changed and another effect that the drug had on him was blanking out his remembrance. In the years that followed he remembered very little that took place the entire year that he was on Valium.

The year had been difficult for me also. There were days when I felt like walking out the door and never coming back. As I thought about this desire, I knew that such a leading would never be of the Lord. I thought about the victory such an act would give to Satan and how it would ruin my life and my ministry. The Lord taught me three great lessons through this experience:

1. I learned that the Lord is my joy. A child of God's joy should not be based upon the actions of others. Nor should it be based upon circumstances.

2. I learned that the Lord is my strength. Many times I had sung Frances Allitsen's sacred song 'The Lord is my Light and my Salvation, Whom, then shall I fear?...The Lord is the strength of my life;...Of whom then, shall I be afraid' taken from the twenty-seventh Psalm. Everytime I sang

the song I believed the words that I was singing but I had never experienced the strength of the Lord in the way that I had the past year. A wife often depends upon her husband's strength and through this experience I learned that the only strength I had was the Lord's.

3. I learned that I needed more compassion and love for my husband. The thing that I had wanted to get away from was his drug induced behavior. My daily prayer became that the Lord would give me more love for my husband. The Lord gave an affirmative answer to this prayer, but it took time.

Through this trying time and through the rest of this school year the words of one song seemed to bless me and would constantly come to mind.

He Giveth More Grace

He giveth more grace when the burdens grow greater;
He sendeth more strength when the labors increase
To added affliction, He addeth His mercy;
To multiplied trials, His multiplied peace.
His power has no boundary known unto men;
For out of His infinite riches in Jesus,
He giveth, and giveth, and giveth again.

When we have exhausted our store of endurance,
When our strength has failed ere the day is half done,
When we reach the end of our hoarded resource,
Our Father's full giving is only begun.
His love has no limit, His grace has no measure,
His power no boundary known unto men;
For out of His infinite riches in Jesus,
He giveth, and giveth, and giveth again.[12]

Only four boys were living in the dorm when we returned from Vancouver. How disappointed we were to learn that two boys had been expelled and others had left due to homesickness.

There were more girl students than boys this year and the staff decided that there should be a dorm switch

---

12. Peterson, Op.Cit. p.35

again. This time Chuck and I were to move with the dorm boys into where Stony, Sarah and the girls had been living.

The move itself was the quickest I had ever experienced. I packed our dishes and linens in boxes but the rest of the furniture was moved by the students. Chuck helped some but since he was still recuperating from the surgery he was not allowed to lift heavy furniture.

On a Saturday morning each student, or two students together, would pick up some piece of furniture, then they would walk past three buildings down the path and place the furniture in our new home. That evening everything was in place. The girls even unpacked the boxes and put the dishes away in the cabinets and the linens away in the closet. There was no interruption in anyone's schedule due to a move.

Our new home had a living room, dining room, kitchen and laundry area. Then three bedrooms and a bath. Chuck and I slept in one bedroom and we had two boys in each of the other two bedrooms.

It seemed like every building, except where the Parkin's and Larry and Ellen Antoine lived had new inhabitants.

The old two room cabin, in which we had lived for a year, now had residents. Sarah and Stoney moved into it. The cabin now had running water along with electricity and propane cook stove. The only convenience that the cabin did not have was a bathtub or shower and Sarah and Stoney went to other homes to take their weekly bath.

On one side of our new living quarters the Parkins lived and on the other side lived Dan and Ginger Work with their two little children.

In the other staff house lived John and Marie Cerwinka, a retired couple who came to do the maintenance work and cooking (except for weekends when the rest of the staff pitched in). Marie became famous for her homemade soups. She saw that there never was a scrap of leftover food that was not used up and often it ended in the soup.

This year the owner of a food store in Prince George had cleared out his walk-in freezer and gave the Native Institute of Canada many frozen food packages. There were small quantities of the vegetables but oodles and oodles of hot dogs and brussel sprouts.

Marie concocted every imaginable hot dog combination possible; boiled, baked and fried hot dogs, cheese dogs, hot dogs in macaroni, hot dogs in soup, hot dogs in stew and even ground hot dogs made into hot dog salad for sandwiches to mention a few of the dishes. Hot dogs were served in quantity at conference times and by Christmas most staff people felt that they could never look at another hot dog. By spring some of the students felt the same way but the majority of the students could eat hot dogs on and on.

The Woodkey's, a young couple with two little girls came to live as dorm parents for the girls. Brenda and Dan Woodkey had been village missionaries for two years before coming to the Native Institute of Canada. The native girls all appreciated the good looking couple who were their new parents.

Larry Antoine and Gerald Tom were part-time students and part-time staff this year. Larry taught the 'Life of Christ' to the high school students for their daily Bible class. Gerald worked as janitor for the A-frame.

The last cabin on the property now had a native family of seven living in it: Fred and Sylvia Raw Eater plus their five children. Dick came to the Native Institute of Canada to attend Bible school and Sylvia monitored a few subjects. Four of their five children went to the grade school in town.

Every building on campus was filled to capacity.

As Dean of Students, Chuck was responsible for all aspects of the students health and welfare. He contacted the dentist and doctors to make appointments and arranged for the students' transportation to town and back to school. Chuck gave permission and coordinated students visits home or elsewhere. All money orders that the students received were cashed for them by Chuck at the Post Office in Quesnel. It became quite a grueling session for Chuck to go through all the questions and the need to prove that he was authorized to cash the money order made out to some other person than himself.

One week Chuck was in the Post Office two different days to cash a money order. He had a different clerk each time. After Chuck had answered about two minutes worth of questions during the second visit, the clerk who had waited on him the previous time realized what was going on. She called, in a very exasperated voice over to the clerk questioning Chuck, 'O Myrtle, just give him the money, don't ask him any more questions.'

As time went by Chuck and Arctic Missions became known in many of the businesses in Quesnel.

Food purchasing had been worked down to a science by now. A wholesale company for case lots had been located in town. Chuck would call the order in the day before and on the day we went to town we just had to pick up the large quantity of staples.

Then the two of us would go to the three food stores in town and write down the prices for vegetables, fruits, meats, eggs, powdered milk, bread, paper products and whatever else needed on the weekly food order. After the prices were compared, a second visit to the three stores would be made to do the purchasing.

Next stop was for the student store supplies - soda, candy and potato chips. Then supplies for the school classrooms and maintenance were picked up. Any other business was taken care of as long as the stores stayed open.

Usually Chuck and I left the Native Institute of Canada

at eight in the morning and returned at eight at night each Friday. Any other trips that Chuck needed to make to town, I stayed home because my teaching schedule was Monday to Thursday.

Student counselling by Chuck and myself took much more of our time this year and the next year than either of the two previous years or the years that followed after these two.

The animistic North American Indian believes that everything has a spirit; trees, animals, the ground, buildings, a human body after death and so on and on. Beside these types of spirits there is also the spirit of anger, the spirit of hate, the spirit of lust, the spirit of bitterness, just to name a few, and a very obvious one in Indian culture, the spirit of fear.

Many a girl would wake at night trembling from a nightmare and I would counsel and pray with her for hours until the fear was gone.

(I believe the fear of the dark, the fear of night sounds and night movements in the bush plus the fears of nightmares are one of the reasons that Indian people do not go to bed until almost morning. As a consequence of this sleep pattern they don't rise until noon.)

It is true that anger, hate, lust, bitterness, fear, etc. are normal human emotions but when they become extremely excessive they pass beyond human normality and become Satanic oppression. Usually some unconfessed sin in the person's life is what gave Satan the stronghold. After the sin was confessed to the Lord the person would become free of the spirit problem.

Students were freed from the problem through counselling and prayer but there were times that we had to deal with demons. A Christian cannot be possessed by a demon but they can be oppressed. The evidence of the problem appears the same since the problem is in the spirit realm.

Chuck nor I had ever experienced this type of thing before. As we dealt with these problems, I kept thinking, 'If I keep this up, I will go crazy.' (I am sure this thought is one of Satan's lies). Then I came across a verse one evening in my devotions that clarified my mind. It was found in second Timothy chapter one verse seven, 'For

God hath not given us the spirit of fear; but of power, and of love, and of a sound mind.'

I realized that God promised me a sound mind ·that I did not need to fear that I would go crazy because of the fact that I was battling Satanic forces.

I also realized that if God did not give the spirit of fear, the only other source that it could come from was Satan.

Then I memorized the verse and quoted it every time I was faced with fear in my own life and encouraged the students to memorize it for the same purpose. The spirit of fear could not stand against the Word of God.

It seemed that for these two years Satan unleashed all of his force against the ministry of the Native Institute of Canada. This had been his territory alone and now his power was in jeopardy. Chuck and I were in the battle many hours and became physically exhausted but we saw the victory of the Lord in a way that we had never seen before.

Another area in which the work of Satan was noticed was the lack of patience and love between the staff during these two years.

God designs missionaries as very strong willed people in order to survive on the field. Often there are frictions between missionaries because of strong wills but usually through love solutions are found. These two years love was not apparent and the staff felt miserable. The undercurrent of the problems affected the lives of the students. They could see in the staff irritability, because of being under too much pressure; bitterness from some who did not want to be at the Native Institute of Canada, while others didn't want to be doing jobs that they were assigned to do; criticism between staff; untruths, backbiting and jealousy. The old nature wanted to reign. Through the grace of God this too eventually was overcome and love again ruled over the majority of staff conflicts.

This fall I was asked to be librarian. The school had been given many books during the summer of nineteen seventy-two. A librarian had visited the campus and had started cataloging books. She left a Dewey decimal system catalog for someone to continue and Sarah took over the job. Sarah had cataloged and put on the library shelves about fifteen hundred books, when she no longer felt she should be doing the job due to the imminent arrival of a baby.

I enjoyed reading but had never done any library work. The job of figuring out the Dewey decimal system and what number to give around two thousand more books seemed almost overwhelming.

Every book that was on the shelf had a three by five file card with information about the book typed on it. The card contained the information about the Dewey decimal number, the author's name, the book title, the subject matter, the publisher and the year of publication. Each book was also give a number in sequence as it was received at the school and this number also appeared on the card.

For several days I would browse through a book to determine the subject matter then go through the Dewey decimal book to find the number for the subject matter, then type the card, label the book and put the book on the shelf. Then I learned that there were supposed to be four file cards for each book. In the past only one card had been typed so that there would be a record of the book but in order to get as many books quickly on the shelves for use, the time wasn't taken to type the other three cards. Now I had fifteen hundred books to type three cards for and two thousand books to catalog and type four cards for. The three other cards that needed to be typed were for the reference files. For the reference files the information on the cards had to be in different orders; one file was listed by authors, the second file by book titles and the third file by subject matter. These files were kept in the library for student use. The card that was already typed was for the master file kept in the office.

Sarah helped with the typing of cards in her home as long as I was librarian. Other staff members, summer workers and some students helped with the typing. I usually spent two hours a day working in the library and typing cards. One hour in the morning at the time when the French class had been previously scheduled and the other hour after school to supervise the typing students whose gratis assignment was to help in the library.

I am not a good typist. I have a fairly fast hunt and peck system using all eight fingers but I have never studied typing. My arthritis would set in my shoulders and neck after about a half hour of typing. I would be stiff and in pain the rest of the day. I am also the type of person who needs to see the completion of a job and librarians never see this. By the end of five years (with a year's furlough in the middle of them) all the books were cataloged and put on the shelves and all the cards had been typed. At this time the Lord sent another staff member to be librarian who enjoyed library work. I knew the Lord had not designed me physically or emotionally for this job and gladly gave the job over.

Chuck and I spent a few days down in the states for a Missionary conference. Usually, after an evening meeting we would be invited to someone's home for refreshments and a time of fellowship. Most of the time the conversation would steer around to our ministry.

One evening Chuck was talking about the survival methods we had learned at Boot Camp because of the possibility of danger due to extreme cold. He mentioned the possibilities of a missionay's car breaking down away in the bush and if the survival methods were not known, the missionary could freeze to death.

One man became concerned that we could become stranded sometime when the temperature was way below freezing. Later he decided to give us a heater that could be used without a motor. He chose a blow torch type run by propane. The man told us that the heater could be placed in the back seat of a vehicle and the people could sit inside and stay warm.

We appreciated the thought but were never able to use the heater that he gave us. The flame shot out for three feet from the nozzle. Anyone sitting in the front seat would have been toasted instead of toasty warm. We were uncomfortable using the heater anywhere because of the open flame and it's intensity.

On extremely cold mornings it was impossible to start a car. If someone needed to travel in the morning a

Coleman camping stove would be lit and placed under the engine part of the car to warm the oil in the block. After the oil became fluid, then the engine would start. Usually it would take a while before the oil warmed and the car owner would go do other things, then come back to start his car.

One such morning Stoney decided to use our blow torch heater in place of the coleman stove. He set it up, then went to do a few things and came back to a smoking engine with all of it's wires burned out.

Native people often laugh when something is accidentally destroyed, so Stoney laughed. Everyone who heard the story about the burned out wires laughed. Then Stoney had to borrow a car to go to town and buy wiring for his engine.

We celebrated Christmas this year at the Native Institute of Canada. Charles and David were home. One other family remained on campus for the holiday and we all had Christmas dinner together.

Our church in Seattle sent us a rug for our living room. It was green shag in twelve inch squares. Chuck and the two boys installed the rug during the holiday. How much nicer our living room looked and it made the area much warmer than before.

This year there were more gospel team trips and more Sunday evening concerts for the choir. Wherever we traveled for these engagements, everyone in the car usually sang going and coming home. One of the favorite choruses for these trips was 'Oh, how I love Jesus, Oh, how I love Jesus, Oh, how I love Jesus because He first loved me.' Then someone in the car would sing, Oh, Mary, do you love Jesus, do you really love Jesus, tell me Mary do you love Jesus because He first loved you. Mary would answer with the first words and then go on to pick someone in the car to sing the second words to. And the song would be sung until everyone had a turn to sing individually about how they loved Jesus.

On one of these trips a new girl was with us. The song was started and when Gloria was asked 'Do you love Jesus?' silenced followed. In a short time someone else was called on and the song went on.

That night Gloria went to one of the staff members and told them of the incident and that she couldn't sing the song because she didn't love Jesus. The staff member had the joy of leading Gloria to a personal relationship with the Lord Jesus Christ. The next time we went on a trip, Gloria's sweet voice responded to the song and she sang, 'Oh, how I love Jesus...because He first loved me.'

Gloria's life had been very typical of many of the girls who attended the Native Institute of Canada. As a baby Gloria had not been wanted by her parents and she had been mistreated. Welfare took her away from her parents and had placed her in several different homes. There too, Gloria had been mistreated. Sometimes she had been so physically abused that she would need to recuperate in a hospital. Seeking love and affection she went to live with a man at an early age. Because drink was so easily available that problem began when she was young.

Gloria was in her mid-teens when a missionary family moved close to her reserve. They had what Gloria was seeking for and she often visited with them. The missionary thought that Gloria had made a decision for Christ when he recommended to her that she go to the Native Institute of Canada for upgrading. But it wasn't until the words of the song were asked of Gloria that she realized that something was lacking in her relationship with God.

Gloria arrived at school shortly before Christmas. Each year at this season we would have a banquet and a gift opening in the A-frame dining hall before the students left for their holiday at home. A Sunday School class that supported Chuck and me would send a large cash gift each year to buy a present for every student. There was just one stipulation, the present had to be a warm piece of clothing.

This gift was the first gift that Gloria had ever received in her life and she did not know how to react. She took it back to her room, put it on a shelf and left it there. Several years later, when Gloria was a Bible School senior, Gloria was giving her testimony and she told about her mixed feelings over getting a gift. Then she shared how she had felt the same way over the gift of salvation. She had not known how to respond and had just 'put it on a shelf' until one day she shared her faith with another person. Then she knew what to do with the gift of salvation. She was to share it.

The Christmas season was never a good one on the reserves and our students usually had a difficult time at home. The true reason for the holiday was not understood by the non-Christian Indian and their only purpose for the holiday was 'partying' and getting drunk. No one ever gave gifts.

After the boys returned from their ten days at home, one of the boys came up to me and asked me how I liked his new jacket. I could see that it wasn't new, but told him that it was very nice. Fred said that he and his cousin wanted to exchange gifts at Christmas time but they had no money to buy gifts. Instead they exchanged jackets. It was a gift of love and Fred was very proud of it.

We had purchased material for each girl to make a long skirt with the money from the Sunday School class. Staff ladies and the girls got together to make the skirts for Sunday and choir use.

The Native Institute of Canada had a ruling that dresses were to be worn to Sunday services until the temperature dropped below minus twenty-five degrees Farenheit. Slacks could then be worn. Now with nice long skirts the cold wouldn't be felt on the legs.

Every Sunday morning Chuck would listen for the official weather temperature on the radio because there was always a call from some female student asking if it would be alright to wear slacks to church. It seemed that the thermometer outside of the girls dorm was always ten degrees colder than any other thermometer.

There was only once an exception made to this rule. One year a woman fifty-three years of age attended Bible School. She had never worn a dress in her life and said she would be embarrassed to have her legs show. She thought she could never wear a dress. The exception was made for her only.

Lewis Holmes did not return to school until the second semester. He had had a difficult spiritual problem all summer and fall.

When Lewis had first gotten home from school last

134

spring, his buddies on the reserve held him down on the ground and poured liquor down his throat until he became drunk. Once tasting the alcohol again, Lewis couldn't resist it. He would drink, get drunk, feel guilty and then go through the whole process again.

The missionary on Lewis' reserve would explain, 'If we confess our sins, he is faithful and just to forgive us our sins, and to cleanse us from all unrighteousness' (I John 1:9) to Lewis but this was incomprehensible to Lewis. On a reserve no one ever confessed anything and no one ever forgave anyone but tried to get even instead. Lewis was too ashamed to confess to God and sure that God would never forgive him. Finally, Lewis gave in to God's requirements and after the confession, the guilt load was lifted. By then a whole semester of school had gone by. Staff and students welcomed Lewis back to school.

One hundred and thirty-seven inches of snow fell on the Native Institute of Canada. It seemed that every day or every night it snowed and there were days when it snowed both day and night. It just piled higher and higher. I loved to watch the snow fall but 'cabin fever' effects began to be felt. This year it affected me with the sense of having no privacy. Being the only woman in the house, one bathroom, hemmed in by snow, I longed for an evening or two where I could soak in the tub for hours and lounge in the living room in my bathrobe and pajamas. As spring advanced the cabin fever diminished.

All year long I had been inspecting the dorm rooms, checking to see if beds were made and rooms straight. I also supervised the clothes washing for the boys dorm. Each boy washed his own clothes and bedding once a week in an assigned washing machine and on an assigned schedule. It began to dawn on me that I hadn't seen some of the boys washing any sheets. I went to check the beds and the sheets were clean. It took me quite a while to figure this one out.

In our culture we put on blankets or take them off depending upon the temperature. We sleep between the sheets with the right amount of blankets on top. These boys were not used to sleeping between the sheets. They made their beds with about five blankets. If it was a warm night they slept between the two top blankets. As the nights got colder they moved down two, three or four blankets. These boys didn't need to wash their sheets but they had to wash all their blankets at the close of school.

**Toward the end of January the staff decided that it was** time for the students to have a break so a retreat was planned.

Our ranching friends out at Nazko offered their homes for the retreat. We left Friday after classes and drove to a home on frozen Rainbow Lake. The temperature was minus forty-five degrees, snow was waist deep and the only way to reach the house where we were to gather was by walking across a lake path and climbing a steep bank.

I did fine walking across the lake but climbing the bank was not very successful. For each step that I would climb up I would slide two back. Then I stepped off the path and landed waist deep in snow. By now I was laughing so hard that I couldn't do anything. All of the students were lined up behind me. Lewis was directly behind me and he decided to help but each time he would push he would draw back in embarrassment because the only portion of my anatomy available for him to push was my derrierre. Then Lewis worked himself into a position where he could put his arms around my waist and lift me up. He turned red from embarrassment, but I was on top of the embankment and everyone else could get up.

Around midnight with starlight to guide us, Chuck and I had to go back down the embankment and across the lake as we were assigned another home in which to sleep. Our bedroom had four bunks, ice on one wall and a puddle of ice on the floor - no heat! But we had lots of warm covers and at breakfast had sweet fellowship with the rancher and his wife.

On this day the students traversed the lake in snow machines and ice skates. A real fun time ended with a barbecue in the basement of the home where we had gathered the night before.

In the middle of winter a full moon, reflecting from the snow, made light as bright as day. One such night we were driving to town and Chuck wondered if it would be bright enough to drive with the car lights off. He turned them off and we drove for a few miles seeing with no difficulty. The moonlight was beautiful on the snow covered trees and ground. The stars were brilliant and the sky was filled with them.

Often when snow fell all day, the snowplow could be heard on the road at ten or eleven o'clock at night. One such night the plow came onto campus and Ginger Work's curiosity got the best of her. She wanted to find out what was going on but was dressed in her night clothes. So she threw a jacket and boots on and snuck out to hide behind a five inch tree trunk. For some reason right at that moment the man on the snow plow turned on his spotlight and it was aimed right at Ginger who went screaming back to her cabin. For quite some time after that, Ginger was kidded by people asking her, 'Do you know who the red haired, pink nightgowned, lady phantom is?'

Since there was always a great deal of work to be accomplished, a person developed a sense that it was wrong to rest or take time off. At a ladies' prayer meeting, Marie shared with the women how that one afternoon after lunch she sat to rest. Then she heard someone approach her front door and the thought came to her head, 'Oh, I have to find something to do, I can't be found just sitting.' So she jumped up to get something in her hand and then realized how ridiculous the idea was. Yet I could empathize with her because I had done exactly the same thing. Such an attitude could easily ruin a missionary's health.

Around Easter time I again felt led to organize a recital. Instead of just the Native Institute of Canada's people having a part in the recital, Quesnel church choirs were invited to sing in 'Quesnel's First Spring Concert.'

The following segments from the editorial carried in the Cariboo Observer written by George Whiteley gives a good summary of the evening's performance:

'The Good Book commands us to 'make a joyful noise unto the Lord.' A hymnbook preface says the church 'has come singing down through the ages.'
Music plays a large part in worship, thanks to the efforts of many people. In smaller places like Quesnel, choir directors, organists and singers work for nothing, as do

other church members. Their counterparts in large places like Vancouver are paid.

I would judge the First Quesnel Sacred Music Festival a success, although it attracted little support. Why, I wonder did it wait for people 35 miles from town to organize it? The festival resulted from a concert given at Christmas by June Temple and Helen Perkins, on the staff of The Native Institute of Canada on Tibbles Road, going to Nazko. It was held in the music room of Correlieu Secondary School.there was a good audience, but most were performers...Eugene Parkins, institute principal, was master of ceremonies, with Brenda Woodkey at the piano for audience singing.

The first group...were seven women from St. John the Divine Anglican Church...The Evangelical Free Church was represented next...the Parkins and their violins joined Mr. Neufeld and his cello for 'I believe in miracles,' after which Catherine Holiday joined Mrs. Parkins at the piano for 'Come thou fount of every blessing' and 'The King of love my shepherd is'...Mrs. Temple sang a prayer of forgiveness, 'O divine Redeemer,' followed by a song of praise from a person who knows he has been forgiven. 'I know that my Redeemer liveth' is from one of the most majestic pieces of church music, 'The Messiah' by Handel. Mrs. Parkins accompanied her.

Six Indian girls and four boys from the Institute sang of the 'Crown of Thorns' given Christ, then picked up the spiritual beat with 'O Sinner Man', featuring percussion accompaniment by Jean Born, St. Catherines, Ontario, and Gerald Tom, Merritt, and closed with 'Holy, Holy' not the well-known hymn, but one featuring the line, 'And we lift our hearts before you as a token of our love.' They were directed by Mrs. Temple, with Mrs. Woodkey at the piano.

Mrs. Parkins and her violin closed the evening with 'The Holy City', Mrs. Haliday was at the keyboard...'

A second fire occurred this spring. Once again it started when everyone was up in the A-frame; this time at a Sunday morning service. When Larry, Ellen and the two girls left for church, they thought the fire was out in the airtight stove, but the draft was open. A spark ignited the wood and the stove became so hot it set the sofa that was next to it on fire.

Rose had returned to the girls dorm after the service and saw that Larry and Ellen's cabin was on fire. This girl was very soft spoken and unexciteable. She returned to the A-frame and quietly said, 'Larry, your cabin is on fire,' Larry laughed and Rose responded, 'Larry, I'm not kidding, your cabin is on fire.' The men rushed down to the cabin but it was too late; they could only stand and watch.

Larry and Ellen lost their clothing and some household possessions. The mission lost the building and the furniture. I'm sure each staff family lost something that they had loaned to Ellen and Larry to use. But the Lord faithfully replenished the lost articles.

The mission moved a mobile home onto the site of Larry and Ellen's cabin and people in town graciously responded to the need supplying clothing, furniture and household items.

Once all the snow melted from the ground, the area needs cleaning up. Things dropped in the snow now lay on the ground. Often things thought lost were found.

Chuck and I cleaned up all the rubbish around the outside of our home and then decided to also get rid of a lot of rocks that were sitting around the lawn. We got a wheelbarrel and filled it with rocks to dump in a gully.

Little three year old Bryan Work was out playing and decided it would be fun to help us load the wheelbarrel. After awhile Bryan was called in to lunch and while he was eating his mother asked him what he had been doing all morning. Bryan answered, 'Playing with Chuck and June.' His mother said, 'and what were you playing?' Bryan answered, 'picking up rocks.'

The choir was singing in a Prince George church evening service. During the announcement time, the Pastor was kidding some with the students. One of the students responded and the Pastor replied, 'Oh, you're pulling my leg.' At this point the student walked across the platform and grabbed the Pastor's leg. Of course, everyone in the congregation laughed, but only those on the platform could see the surprised look on the student's face at being laughed at.

This is a perfect example of how many native mind patterns think in a literal process. Many of the abstract phrases that the white culture uses have no understandable meaning to the native mind.

We had been praying for a new car for nearly two years. At first sporadically, as we realized that the car was wearing out. Then daily, as we saw that soon our car would not go at all without major repairs.

Within a few months the Lord provided us with two cars. He is always so abundant in His giving. A young man concerned about our need for a car reconditioned a nineteen sixty-five Pontiac sedan and gave it to us. Landgren Church gave us a new Pinto station wagon. The Pinto was designated for our own personal use. We used the Pontiac for all the trips to town on mission business and to take the gospel teams on their trips.

When Chuck went into the government building to licence and register the two cars, both times he put down the car as a gift and did not cost us anything. The clerk would always shake her head and say, 'People don't give away cars.'

Shortly after spring break-up individuals and youth groups began arriving to help with the summer's building plans. The first thing that needed to be done was shovel and pick work under the A-frame. It was time to finish off the basement but it had been found that the floor was not deep enough and needed to be dug out about two feet.

One youth group accomplished this in a week's time in early June. A group of men, who were accomplished loggers, came for a week and finished the next project which was a large shop building made out of logs. The men even made notched log corners on the building.

The huge, three-bay building made maintenance work much easier, especially in cold weather.

One bay was for auto mechanics, another bay housed power tools. When school was in session the shop class received their instructions in these two areas. The third bay was used for storage.

When it came time to place the water pipes in the ground to connect the house plumbing to the well and sewerage, a hole six feet deep had to be dug. Frost went almost six feet deep in the winter time and in order to not have water freeze in the pipes, they had to be placed below the frost line.

Each summer there was a concern that some unsuspecting summer worker would drive some heavy equipment (including cars) over the ground which could cause a stone to puncture the plastic pipe six feet below. If that happened, another six foot deep hole would have to be dug to repair the pipe.

Leaks happened twice. One time when the backhoe was broken and only Chuck and Dan Work were on campus. Two men with bad backs dug the six feet manually. After that, the phrase 'don't drive in front of the cabins' (since that was where the pipes were placed) was often heard in the summertime.

To keep the pipes from freezing above ground, electric heat tapes were wrapped around the pipes. They were kept plugged in day and night.

One time when a leak occurred and the water had to be turned off, the automatic shut-off on the heat tape didn't work. The heat melted the plastic pipe and when the water was turned back on a waterfall occurred in our basement. I was working upstairs and kept wondering why I heard water running. I first checked the bathrooms and then went down to the basement. Six inches of water covered the mud floor and more was cascading down from the pipes above my head.

All water to all cabins was shut-off to repair the leak since the cabins did not have separate shut-off valves. (Every time a leak happened it was suggested that separate valves would be good).

Another phenomenon of our water system was the fact that each cabin down the line had less water pressure. Especially in the morning, when everyone first woke and were using bathroom and cooking facilities. Some mornings it seemed like it took fifteen minutes to fill the coffeepot with enough water to make two cups of coffee.

With these projects completed, the main building project began. That was the addition of a dorm wing on our home.

A man came up from the states to supervise the

construction. We were away from the Native Institute of Canada for a month to attend a Missionary Conference in Alaska and also the birth of our second grandchild. When we left the campus, the flooring and a part of the log walls of the dorm wing had been constructed. On returning home the dorm was completed and it had been built on the open dorm concept plan.

The entrance from our home to the dorm was through the laundry. The entryways outside and the one to our home, the bathroom and five bedrooms encircled a lounge area. This open living plan proved very enjoyable for the fellows.

The gentleman, who had overseen the construction of the dorm, and his wife felt led of the Lord to become missionaries with Arctic Missions in Canada.

Canadian Immigration refused this couple entrance to work in Canada. At this point Chuck and I began to feel the need of making Canadian Bible School students and Canadian church people aware of Arctic Missions need for missionaries. If it was going to become harder for Americans to come minister in Canada, then the native people would have to be reached by Canadians.

Charles and David were not home this summer. Charles had remained in the east for summer employment. He had met a certain young lady who seemed very important who also lived in the east. I am sure there must have been some connection between the young lady and his decision to stay east.

David went on a summer missionary training program with Northern Canada Evangelical Mission. He was ministering in northern Saskatchewan at the very remote Indian village of Ile a la Crosse.

## Chapter IX

Anyone interested in wildlife would enjoy living in the Baker Creek area.

During winter months, when snow piles high on each side of the road there were quite a few times when a moose would appear on the road in front of the car and he would gallop in his gangly-gait in front of the car.

Naturally, we would creep along not wanting to terrify the animal but his innate fear would make him trot along with his legs pumping in an odd cadence. So he would continue until a break in the snowbank came or a side lane appeared for him to turn off.

Certain times of the year a small herd of deer would graze near the road and when our vehicle approached they would bound off into the woods.

The bear population varied from year to year. We saw only black bears but east of Quesnel and southwest of town, grizzly bears would sometimes be sighted and any problems would be reported in the newspaper.

One year, Pauline and Denny were visiting in the early summer. Midmorning, Pauline and I decided to take a little walk and as we strolled past the area where the school kept their garbage (until it was hauled to the dump) Pauline asked me what the holes all over the cans came from. I nonchalantly said that the holes were from bear teeth. Pauline quietly said under her breath, 'Come on feet, let's go' and her knees rose like pistons in an engine in high gear. As the implications of what I said sank into my mind, my short, stubby legs were right behind Pauline's.

Another year when we had quite a few bear sightings, Chuck and I were out for an evening stroll along the side of the creek flowing through the school's property. We kept hearing a rustling in the bushes and would look at each other with only one thought - 'it's a bear.' Finally we heard a loud crash and a loud splash into the creek and

Chuck called out, 'Is that you David?' in hopes that our son was playing a joke on us. It wasn't David, it wasn't a bear, but a huge beaver, just one of many who swam in Baker Creek.

For several years we lived in one of the staff homes where the creek flowed about twenty feet from our living-room and dining room windows. We enjoyed watching beaver and muskrat swimming either upstream or downstream.

The loons with their haunting calls, and ducks would often build their spring nests along the banks and it was fun to watch the baby ducklings mature. As the geese traveled north they too would stop to rest along the creek bed. It seemed that there was always something interesting to watch from the windows of this house.

Along the creek there was evidence in many spots where beaver had been at work. There were half chewed through trunks where the beaver had changed his mind concerning that particular tree and still it stood erect. There were also huge felled trees where the beaver had finished his chopping and then chewed off branches to drag back to his dam. Little piles of wood chips were left where the beavers' handiwork had taken place.

When the beavers became over-populated, they caused problems for the ranchers. As the creek becomes more and more dammed, the water would back up into the grazing land for cattle. Then the rancher would search for the dams to destroy them.

The trappers who lived close by usually did well with beaver pelts. They were thick and of good quality.

One evening when Chuck and I were out for a walk, a rancher-trapper neighbor drove alongside of us in his truck and stopped to chat. He said 'want to see something ugly?' and walked to the back of the truck. There under the tarp was a nude beaver. The pelt had been removed. The flesh was exposed. Bucky beavers teeth really protrude when there is no fur and it truly is an ugly sight.

Some of the trappers eat the meat which is dark in color but we never tasted it.

Quite often a potluck dinner would be held in the A-frame dining hall on campus. To one of these a muskrat dish was brought. Everyone thought it was good as long as they didn't know what they were eating. After the meal was over the dishes meat content was announced. Noses turned up and groans could be heard all over the room. The Indian couple who had brought the dish had a good chuckle.

Early each spring, a family of Osprey would nest in the same tree every year. The tree was on an island in Tibbles Lake but at a spot easily seen from shore.

A few miles east, near Penchesicut Lake, an eagle family returned each year. Their nest was easily seen from the road to town.

One summer, Chuck and David were out on Penchesicut Lake fishing for rainbow trout and saw quite an aerial display. The osprey had flown over the lake, swooped down and brought up a fine, plump trout. But the eagle had caught sight of this and came to claim the fish. A battle in the sky followed and the two men lay back in the canoe to watch. After much butting and swooping neither bird got the fish. It fell from the osprey's talons into the water before the eagle could retrieve it. Both birds headed for their nests.

These majestic birds could often be seen soaring over the Native Institute of Canada's campus. Once in awhile one would plummet into Baker Creek and rise with a twelve to fourteen inch trout. The bird's fish always seemed larger than any Chuck or I ever caught in the creek.

The raven was another bird native to the area and seen year round. During the summer months robins, camp robbers and thousands of barn swallows made the campus buildings their homes. It was surprising to also see a few hummingbirds each summer and many staff homes had their feeders. Never thought this little creature traveled so far north.

The robins usually arrived while there was still snow on the ground and Chuck would usually remark 'they forgot their snowshoes' each time we'd look out the window and see their feathers all ruffled out trying to keep warm.

The three animals who arrived on campus with us

lived a good many years. One female cat belonged to Charles and had been given to him for his birthday in 1966. She was multi-colored, shorthaired and a very good mouser. Her name was Topper. Topper had had several litters of kittens before we left Seattle but when we arrived at Baker Creek there were no male cats within miles. We had no kittens for several years but when the Longs moved down the road from us, they brought a male cat with them. Within a few months a litter of kittens arrived. The girls in the dorm enjoyed watching the kittens grow. When they were big enough we took them to town to find homes for them. While we were gone Topper ran away and we never saw her again.

As long as Topper was in the home we never had any field mice visit us. She would often deposit a dead one on our doorstep that she had caught during the night. One time she ran into our cabin with a flying squirrel in her mouth. I screamed and jumped on the table, but soon realized that I should have crawled under the table because as Charles and David chased the cat, she dropped the squirrel and it took to the air. Then the boys took brooms and tried to swat the squirrel down while I stood on the table screaming and the flying animal circled my head. If any neighbors had been passing by they would have surely thought that someone was being murdered in our cabin. The squirrel was finally captured and released outside.

Topper not only liked mice, moles and squirrels, but also the huge horseflies that plagued summer workers.

When a cabin reached the stage where the windows and doors were installed the men sprayed the rooms with insect spray. We did not realize it, but Topper was present once when the rooms were sprayed. Not only did she breathe the fumes, but she also ate quite a few of the dead flies. Topper was able to walk home, and then fell over in a stupor. She stayed in a coma for forty-eight hours. Pauline and Patti cried for forty-eight hours thinking that the cat was going to die. When Topper woke, life continued on for her just as if she had been Rip VanWinkle.

The other cat we had was a neutered pure white angora persian that we called Fluffy. I adopted him when he was about two years old and he lived for ten years at the Native Institute of Canada. Fluffy was a very gentle, quiet, dumb cat who did not know that he was supposed to stalk smaller creatures.

There was only one incident in his life when he ever captured anything. It was a bird and just after Fluffy caught it, a summer worker walked by and said, 'What do you have, Fluffy?' Fluffy opened his mouth to answer his distorted 'meow' and the bird flew away.

Fluffy's only purpose in life was to be held and to be petted. He died of old age.

Our dog, Chief, was a mixed springer and cocker spaniel. His bottom jaw was that of the smaller dog and his top jaw that of the larger. He lived with an inch and a half overbite. Patti had gotten him as a puppy but he became David's dog and followed him everywhere when Patti went to college.

David loved to walk in the woods and Chief would always be at his side. One winter when the coyotes were especially prevalent, David decided to see if he could creep up near them but knowing how they lured dogs to eat them he told Chief to stay home.

David followed the coyote tracks in the snow on the frozen creek and when he thought he was close he sat quietly on the bank in the bushes to wait for them to walk up the creek. After a while, David sensed a presence in back of him, and he thought, 'The coyotes have circled in back of me and I'm gone', but there quietly sitting was Chief, and David hugged him in relief.

Chief had a broken tail (he had been hit by a car) and could not wag it. One of the missionaries thought he was a dangerous dog because he never wagged his tail until we explained why. We learned that a dog uses his tail for balance when swimming. We saw Chief almost drown twice. He couldn't keep his back end up in the water.

After Chuck had his back operation, he was told to take a walk daily. So he joined me in my afternoon walk. We always had several dogs walk with us. Always Chief and usually the Work's dog, Trixie, when they lived on campus. Trixie was a large collie who had several meetings with the campus porcupine. She often needed the quills removed from her nuzzle. A neighbor rancher's dog would also join us.

When the Woodkey's were on staff, their big black dog joined us for the walk also. We did not always go at the same time but the dogs seemed to always sense when we were ready and joined right in. The Woodkey's dog loved to chase rocks and Chuck would throw them in all directions and the dog would run after it and bring it back; up over snowbanks, out into the meadow or into the icy creek water. One time Chuck threw the stone ahead of the dog on the roadway. It hit a rock and bounced backward striking the dog in the nose. He never joined us again for a walk.

Believe it or not, every once in a while Fluffy would follow after us so we made quite a menagerie walking on Tibbles Road.

Most of the staff were city bred people and we had cattle at the school. Chuck learned much! Each February, March and April, calves would arrive. During the early months there was always danger of the calf freezing after birth and then some calves had to be pulled.

One shock that Chuck, as a city person, would ever remember, was how a rancher made a pregnancy test for a calf. Perry Jones would often drive the five miles from his cabin to help with any medical problems that the school's livestock might have. He was the one who made the pregnancy test. When Chuck saw Perry shove his hand into the cow's vagina and continue moving inward until his arm was up to his armpit, Chuck was very happy that he was not called to be a rancher.

One March everyone thought a pregnant cow was going to calve, so the men kept watch during the night. Chuck drew the two to four a.m. watch so he went up to the pitch black A-frame which was the closest building to the cow and every twenty minutes went out and looked at the cow who was laying under a tree chewing her cud. He thought, 'I never expected in all my life to be a midwife to a cow.' Here the cow wasn't even in labor and it was several weeks before she delivered.

Another year a cow disappeared in the middle of winter. The staff men went out on foot, on snowshoe, on horseback and even in an airplane looking for the animal. She could not be found until spring came and the ice on the creek melted. She was found floating on the creek. During the winter months she had walked out on the ice and gone through.

If a cow becomes mired in mud it will become exhausted and die. That too, happened. After the spring break-up there were usually several muddy areas, and the cows would often graze close to them. One evening a yearling steer didn't return to the barn, so Dan, Gene, Chuck and David went out looking. Sure enough, it was mired in the mud, but still alive. The men carried the animal back to the barn and it revived, but the very next day it went out to the same spot and did not survive.

We always kept our cattle on the property in the summer when other ranchers had the right to let theirs graze on the open range. Every once in awhile a few of ours would jump the fence and then we'd have to separate them from the other cattle and get them home.

One evening when we took our walk, we came upon the school's cows out on the road. As soon as the cows saw us, they took off into the woods and Chuck was right behind them. When he caught up to them deep in the woods, they were grazing and he sat on a stump to catch his breath. After he sat a few minutes something told him to turn around. There was a cow with horns down, charging him. He stood, waved his arms and the cow stopped. Chuck and I had quite a time getting the cows home.

Sometimes the cows would jump the fence and get into the garden. They caused pure havoc. One day David looked out our window just as a cow ate the last of the cabbages in the Woodkey's garden. That was the end of their garden for that year. No matter how carefully the fence was examined, a cow always seems to be able to find a weak spot to get through.

David was the hunter in the family. We all enjoyed target practice, but David brought home the bacon, so to speak.

When David was twelve, he received his first gun for Christmas, a single shot twenty-two. Then when we moved to Canada, we were given a high powered rifle and another twenty-two.

Grouse were plentiful and David saw to it that we often had 'chicken' as the Indians called it, to eat. It did taste very much like chicken.

One fall one of the dorm fellows came running in to tell us that there was a grouse outside of the dorm door. David grabbed his gun and ran down the hall, and quietly out the door. Chuck counted the shots, there were six in all, and then said, 'how embarrassed David must be to miss all those times with the fellows watching.' Then David walked in carrying five grouse. Not just one bird was out back, but a whole flock.

We only had duck once. It was our first year at the Native Institute of Canada. David brought the duck into our little cabin and I said, 'I do the cooking; its the hunter's job to clean the bird.' So David went outside and cleaned the duck. Right then and there he decided the odor was too obnoxious and he shot no more ducks. Grouse do not have the bad odor when cleaned.

Chuck and I encountered the foul odor once. Larry shot five ducks. He came over with Ellen to find out how to remove the feathers and clean the birds. Ellen had prepared 'chickens' but never ducks. So we got the boiling water and the four of us began pulling feathers. Our kitchen looked like a ripped pillow with little feathers floating in the air. Then Larry and Ellen began opening the cavities to remove the entrails, and Chuck and I ran gasping for air to the door. Larry and Ellen had a good chuckle over the queasy stomached white people.

The Bays family, who had been missionaries in Alaska for over fifteen years moved down to British Columbia to become members of the Native Institute of Canada's staff in the fall of 1975.

John and Marie Cerwinka did not return to be on staff and the Bays moved into the house that the Cerwinkas had vacated.

Wally's position was dean of Education and Alice was a registered nurse (thank goodness). She also taught home economics. Their three teenage daughters joined the Parkins' daughters in attending school in Quesnel.

The new Dean of Education had been investigating the 'Accelerated Christian Education' curriculum and felt that this type of education would adapt to native needs. The program was set up for the high school classes.

Doug and Marjorie Stone were again on staff and were living in the cabin next to our dorm. The Stones had finished their year at Bible School.

Wally, Marjorie and I attended the Accelerated Christian Education training course for supervisors (teachers) at the end of August. We were prepared for classes to begin right after Labor Day, Marjorie was to supervise the morning two hour session in the learning center (classroom) with the students concentrating on science and mathematics in the morning. I had the afternoon two hour session and concentrated on English and Social Studies. These were the four main courses studied through the Accelerated Christian Education program. A few students studied commercial subjects (typing, bookkeeping, etc.) through the Accelerated Christian Education program. The other subjects were taught in the regular classroom style -Home Economics, Art, Bible and Music.

The girls dorm had every bed filled making ten girls

for both high school and Bible School. The dorm parents again were the Woodkeys.

Dan and Ginger Work with their two children had moved down to the trailer where Larry and Ellen had lived after the fire. The Antoines moved to the log cabin next to the trailer. Larry was on staff as a teacher and did not take any classes this school year.

Stoney and Sarah moved to Edmonton, Alberta to minister in a downtown mission for the winter months.

In the old cabin there now lived an Eskimo couple, James and Elizabeth Karetak. James was one of the Eskimo boys who lived in our dorm in the year nineteen hundred and seventy-two. He was now married, had a little girl who was with them, and decided that he should come back and finish Bible School.

Our dorm had five boys in it, four in high school and one in Bible School. One of the high school boys, Dan Webster, had attended the Native Institute of Canada before but he had been expelled when Chuck was down in Vancouver for the back operation. Dan had a likeable personality but was always deliberately doing something he should not be doing. He was also purposefully destructive of property.

Dan had been adopted as a baby by white parents. His pastor father and his mother greatly desired that Dan should know and love the Lord. The school staff had accepted him back in the hope that they could help him. It always seemed though that instead of Dan being helped, he led the other three high school boys into trouble.

Constantly the Bible school student, Art Dick, complained about Dan's noise in the dorm after 'lights out'. Other times Art could not study because of Dan's interruptions. We decided to move Art into one of the bedrooms in our part of the house to get him away from the younger high school fellows.

To Chuck and myself, the most troubling aspect of Dan's behaviour was the uncertainty of his spiritual relationship with Christ. If it was to his advantage, he would say he was a Christian, but he would just as quickly deny being a Christian if that would benefit him.

Late one mid-September afternoon, Wally pounded on

our living room door and hearing me yell 'Come in' (the usual procedure at the Native Institute of Canada) he burst in to ask me if I would drive my husband to town. Chuck needed to go to the doctors because he had badly injured his finger on the table saw while making book shelves for the boys in the dorm. The saw had removed all the flesh under the nail of the index finger on his left hand.

The doctor put Chuck in the hospital right away for a skin graft and released him the next day. He was told to return in ten days. Each day at home the finger became more painful and he went in to the doctors in less than ten days to learn that the finger was badly infected. The skin graft had not taken and the finger was three times it's normal size. For six weeks Chuck was on antibiotics and in and out of the hospital. The doctors felt after six weeks that the end of his finger to the first joint needed to be removed and the surgery was done.

Through the pain and the problems taking place in the dorm, Chuck was driven into the Word more than usual. While meditating in Proverbs, he came across the twenty-second chapter, verse ten and read, 'Cast out the scorner, and contention shall go out; yea, strife and reproach shall cease.' Chuck knew he had found the answer to the problem in the dorm because Dan was a scorner. He scorned all that the Native Institute of Canada stood for, he scorned the Lord Jesus Christ and he scorned the Word of God.

It was necessary again to ask Dan to leave the Native Institute of Canada. After he left, contention and strife were no longer felt in the dorm or classroom and reproach against the name of the school ceased. The Word of God was actively demonstrated before our eyes. The school now understood its inability to cope with young people not yielded to the Lord. Through it all I wondered if Chuck would have been spared the pain he had gone through if Dan Webster had not been reaccepted as a student.

Piano, voice and guitar lessons continued to be held in my living room. A general music class began this year for all students. This class was held in the A-frame. I received information that a travelling opera company was going to perform Puccine's 'La Boheme' in English in

Prince George and decided that going to see the opera would be a good field trip for the music class. We had preliminary study in class of the history and form of opera and listened to a few of the famous arias.

Two of the staff families owned vans, therefore we only needed the two vehicles to make the trip to Prince George, Chuck and I rode with seven students in Dan Woodkey's van with Dan driving. We all had sack suppers since we left the school at four thirty p.m. The night was exceptionally dark and suddenly there loomed in the head- lights of the van a huge bull moose. Everyone held their breath because you never know which way a moose is going to turn; into a vehicle or away from it. We swerved around the moose and continued on up the road. I had to chuckle to myself, wondering who else could say, 'We barely averted hitting a moose on our way to the opera.'

Some of the students had not wanted to go on the trip; they thought opera would be boring. The perform- ance was good and the singers articulated the words plainly enough to be understood. Most of the students' written reports showed that they had enjoyed the produc- tion. The rest said, 'It was better than I expected it to be.'

Wally also had been a music major and chose to lead the choir this year. At first I was very disappointed over no longer directing the choir. It was the one class that I en- joyed teaching and leading over any other. The outreach into the community through this group was a blessing to me. But by the end of the school year, I saw the Lord's wisdom in the decision and never cared to have the work and responsibility of a choir again.

The A.C.E. method of teaching did prove very good for the students. Our young people were tested and placed in each subject at the level that they understood, and progressed from there. Then each student would set their own goals and work at their own pace. The public school records from the early years of education of these stu- dents showed that they had a tendency to give up studying rather than competing with other students' grades. There was no need for competition in the Accelerated Christian Education school but incentives were offered to set high goals within individual progress.

Five evenings a week the high school students were required to attend study hall in the learning center. The study hall was monitored by male staff members and each man averaged one night a week for this duty.

I thought the time was ripe to begin a Bible study among the ladies in Baker Creek community. We studied the book of John. For the first few weeks, there was a good attendance to the class, but as the weather became colder the attendance decreased.

When the ladies reached the third chapter of John and we read aloud the eighteenth verse, 'He that believeth on him is not condemned: but he that believeth not is condemned already, because he had not believed in the name of the only begotten Son of God' one young woman said, 'My, there can't be anything clearer than that.' This young woman accepted the Lord that week.

By December the weather had become bad and the three women who regularly attended the Bible study decided that it would be best to wait until spring to continue the classes.

MacDonalds' Restaurant came to Prince George. Naturally we were anxious to try the Canadian version of the American company. The Christmas season arrived and we needed to drive to Prince George to pick up Charles and David at the airport. So all four of us stopped at MacDonalds before we came home.

The hamburgers were the same in taste (not in price) but when the coke was drunk, we had a different reaction than ever before. Chuck opened his mouth to say something and out came a tremendous burp. Everyone in the place started laughing, but the real punch line came from the next booth. A high child's voice piped up, 'That you, Dad?' That became a standard phrase in our family afterwards whenever anyone burped.

After Christmas break, Chuck and I decided to drive David back to school. The road from the Native Institute of Canada to Prairie Bible Institute travels through the beautiful, famous Canadian Rockies. In winter Jasper is filled with people on ski holidays and the road south to Banff is desolate. As you leave Jasper there is a sign telling the distance to the next gas station. Our tank was three-fourths full and Chuck thought we would have no problem traveling the distance. We were thoroughly enjoying the majestic snow covered peaks and had traveled a good portion of the way when we saw a herd of elk on the mountainside. Chuck, David and I were all staring at the mighty creatures and the car landed in a snow bank. It was very cold and we kept the engine running for heat. Before we knew it the engine sputtered and stopped. No more gas! We wondered if we were going to have to use our survival training that we had learned at Boot Camp. After a while a truck came along and stopped. The driver had a chain and pulled us out of the snowdrift. We waited another while and a second truck came along and stopped. They had a can of gas and offered us some which was just enough to get us to the gas station fifty miles down the road.

When people live in a remote area, they always stop to help anyone in trouble on the road. They know that a life could be in jeopardy in such extreme cold and sometime it could be their own life, so the road code is to help any stranded vehicle. Sometimes in our lives I feel that the help we have received on the road has been angelic.

John Parkins was now in school. He was going through the stage where several mornings he would say he was sick. Then after the school bus had left for school John was no longer sick. One such morning, John's mother thought he really was sick and let him stay home. Then when she found out he wasn't sick, and it was our day to go to town, Helen asked us to drop John off at school.

All the way to town John chattered about his family and about things at home. As we drove up to the school yard, children were playing there and John said, 'Oh, there's Albert, he's my best friend,' Chuck asked John how he knew Albert was his best friend. John's answer was, 'Because every time Albert sees me, he grabs me around the neck and chokes me.' Chuck and I had a good laugh over that.

From time to time I would think about how Chuck and I were missing out on seeing the growth of our grandchildren. Then the Lord would remind me of how blessed we were to be able to share in the lives of so many 'adopted' grandchildren in the other staff families. There were babies and little children in the Antoines, Karetaks, Nicklies, Woodkeys and Work's families, all of whom we held in our arms and played with. We had babysat and enjoyed the Parkins children. All of these children were separated from their grandparents and in a sense we were filling in the role.

Before Christmas, Chuck and I took a gospel team of two girls five hundred miles north to the Fort St. John area. One of the girls with us, Jean Born, was going to see her natural mother for the second time in her life; the first being just six months before.

The Born family were Christian white people who had adopted Jean. Before Jean had been adopted she had lived in sixteen different foster homes and she believed that her mother had given her away because she didn't want her. Jean had a very bitter attitude which affected her whole personality. She was always seeking knowledge about different Indian tribes trying to find out where she belonged. With all the young people from the Blackfoot tribe at school, Jean was always trying to identify with them. Jean did not look like a Blackfoot.

Jean's adopted Aunt and Uncle, the Abe Borns, moved to the Fort St. John area. In their living room they had a picture of the Native Institute of Canada's choir with Jean in it. One evening a Wycliffe translator was in the home of the Borns and looked at the picture. The missionary said that Jean looked like one of the girls in the Beaver tribe where he worked.

Abe and the missionary investigated the records and learned that Jean was a cousin to the Beaver girl. The true story about Jean's separation from her parents was uncovered.

Jean had been born prematurely and had to stay in the hospital for three months. During this time the doctors discovered that Jean's mother had tuberculosis and was placed in a sanitarium. Welfare took over the care of the infant and placed Jean in the homes of white people living in the Fort St. John area for the next three years. Then somehow someone moved away with Jean and no trace of her could be found.

Jean's mother was cured and returned home to find that her baby was missing. For fifteen years the mother had asked every person who went to town to look for a strange Indian girl and ask her if her name was Mary Jean. The loss so affected Jean's mother that she had to spend time in a mental institution.

When Abe Born learned all this information he invited Jean to visit. Jean met her mother, brother and sisters. Her father was deceased. She learned that her father had been chief of the reserve and her brother was to become chief.

What a transformation took place in Jean's personality when she learned all this. Now, with us, Jean was to again visit the Beaver tribe and see her mother. When the two came face to face they threw their arms around each other and the tears streamed down their faces. They could not talk with each other because Jean could only speak English and her mother could only speak the Beaver tongue. Jean's brother was able to translate so they were able to communicate through him. She learned that no one in her family knew the Lord even though a Wycliffe translator had been working with them for thirteen years. Jean had a great burden to reach her family for the Lord.

Chuck and I met Jean's family, including aunts, uncles and cousins and we visited in their homes for an afternoon. We also met some of the white women who had cared for Jean before she left the area. Then we met church people who had been ready to stop supporting the Wycliffe missionary because they had not seen any fruit from his ministry. But these people changed their minds after seeing the lives of our two students. They decided that winning native people to the Lord was worth the cost.

Charles brought home 'the special ladyfriend' from the east and we met Bonnie Loux for the first time. We, too, fell in love with her. David was home for the holiday. Pauline and Denny were able to celebrate with us also and we all had a grand family time together.

Bonnie bought a heavy snow suit before coming to Canada because Charles had told her how cold the weather usually became at that time of the year. The bright red suit was never worn because Christmas week the temperature never got below freezing. Everyone kidded Bonnie about the 'Santa Claus snowsuit' that was never worn.

The weather turned bitter cold right after the students returned from the Christmas vacation. Chuck and I were scheduled to take the three Bible School students on a gospel team trip. Although the roads were bad and there was much snow, the travel to the missionary's home at Chilanko Falls presented no problem.

It was forty-five below zero when we arrived at Wanda and Ralph Browning's house (the missionaries). Two of our students, Gloria and Rose, were to sleep at the Brownings and the two of us plus Art were to sleep in the guest house. Upon our late afternoon arrival, we saw that the fire had not been started in the guest house. We started it right away.

That evening the students with Ralph and Wanda had a meeting in one of the homes. Chuck and I stayed at the Brownings house, read and cranked on an ice cream freezer. For no apparent reason I glanced up and in every window native faces were peering in at us watching what we strange white people were doing. Some were familiar faces from when we lived at Chilanko Forks for boot camp training, others were new faces.

Ralph and Wanda returned home to get the ice cream and took it back to the meeting for refreshments. They were surprised to find that most of the natives wouldn't eat it. To them ice cream was either too sweet or too cold. They preferred the Indian ice cream made from bitter berries, not this kind of stuff.

When we returned for the night's sleep at the guest house it felt like we were walking into a freezer. The airtight heater was blazing away but hadn't penetrated any of the cold. Chuck and I had two down quilts that we slept between and were so toasty warm. Art opted to sleep curled around the stove rolled up in blankets.

The next day, Wanda, Rose and Gloria visited with the Indian ladies. Ralph, who was a pilot, Chuck and Art flew in Ralph's plane out to an area to visit a family that was isolated for the winter.

When they reached the cabin Ralph zoomed over it and then flew to the frozen lake to land. The plane was equipped with skis for such landings. As they approached the lake, Ralph said to Chuck, 'Do you see any overflow?' Chuck said he didn't so Ralph landed. Chuck and Art jumped out of the plane into eighteen inches of slush, which is overflow that sometimes builds up on top of the ice on lakes. Overflow is caused by the ice sinking a few inches below the surface of the water and snow building up on top of the water. It is hard to discern from the air and dangerous to land on because the airplane's skis immediately freeze into the slush and the people in the plane could be stranded until spring break-up.

Ralph's plane skis were frozen and his primary concern was to get off the lake. Ralph told Chuck and Art to lift the plane's tail while he gunned the engine. Nothing happened. They tried it several more times, still nothing happened. Then Ralph said, 'this time try to wiggle the plane back and forth while I gun the engine.' The plane broke free and zoomed across the lake like a bullet until Ralph found a spot that was free of overflow on which to stop. Then Ralph waved for Chuck and Art to come and they plowed through the slush to get there. Chuck thought that Art and he were going to end up with pneumonia from being wet to the knees and standing behind the prop which produced a windchill factor of several hundred degrees below zero. They never even got a sniffle from it.

The plane was sluggish as it took off from the lake and Art's eyes got bigger and bigger as he watched the tree tops get closer and closer. They just barely cleared the trees due to the weight added by many inches of ice frozen to the skis.

As the plane banked and turned they could see a wagon approaching the lake with the native family in it waving for the plane to come back. Ralph said that the family would never understand why they didn't stay and that they would wonder what they had done to offend Ralph enough to cause him to leave. Chuck could only think of the perfect pictorial example of spiritually lost people sitting in a wagon waving for someone to come tell them about the Lord Jesus Christ and no one to tell them. He could not get the picture out of his mind.

The gospel team was taken further west to Anaheim Lake where Chuck and I had been for a well-remembered camping trip while we were at Boot Camp. The mission now had a missionary family located there and they arranged for the team to share at a meeting in their home that evening. We drove back to Chilanko Forks the next morning and planned on leaving for the Native Institute of Canada the following day.

Since the temperature was still down in the minus forty-five to minus fifty degree range, Chuck knew that he would never be able to get the car started unless the block heater was plugged in. The weather station had electricity so Chuck drove the car over there and plugged in the heater. He hoped to get an early start in the morning.

We were packed and ready to go the next morning when Chuck returned from the weather station without the car. Someone had unplugged the car during the night and Chuck had just replugged it. This meant that we could not leave for several hours because it took that long for the heater to bring the block to a temperature where the engine would start.

When the engine did turn over, the frozen speedometer cable registered that we were driving ninety miles an hour in first gear. The drive home was not uneventful. At one place we did an unplanned hundred and eighty degree turn on the ice and then we got stuck in a snowbank. But no one was injured nor was the car damaged and we returned safely to the Native Institute of Canada.

The second semester began with four more young men registered for Bible School. We now had eight fellows in the dorm and they were most enjoyable to work with.

One young man was in his early thirties and had just made a decision for the Lord before he came to school. Everything that he learned in class he became excited about. One day he walked into our living room and said, 'Did you know that Jesus walked on the water? He really walked on the water!' It was refreshing to witness this

161

excitement. How complacent we become to the miracles of Christ the more Christians mature.

February, cabin fever month, had arrived once more and the ladies of the mission decided to counteract the problem by going on a retreat. We all met in Williams Lake on a Friday evening to have dinner and spend a night in a motel. The men babysat at home. A nice restaurant was chosen for dinner and then we all congregated in one of the motel rooms to chat, share experiences (good and bad) and sing.

The next morning after breakfast we had a Bible study and prayer time. Through this effort each woman missionary grew to love and understand her fellow missionary in a deeper way. After lunch we all visited stores to brouse around or shop, then headed for home. The retreat was such a blessing that it was voted to take place each February.

Later the men decided that because the women had had such a good time, they wanted to have a retreat also. They chose the fall for their retreat time and also planned one from year to year because they were refreshed by the time together.

A young peoples' group came up to the school during their spring break. They were helpful around campus in many ways. Because snow was still on the ground, in their spare time the youth group had great fun on snow machines out in the meadow. Their leader returned from one ride and realized that his wallet had fallen out of his back pocket. Everyone started searching but no one found it. The wallet contained three hundred dollars for the youth group's return trip.

The Native Institute of Canada loaned the money to the group when it was time for them to return home. Everyone kept praying that the wallet would be found. After the snow melted one of the students was walking in the meadow and found the money stuffed wallet. Everyone rejoiced here at the Native Institute of Canada and down at the youth group's church.

Chuck and I only experienced snow mobile riding once. Pauline and Denny were visiting us. We were all invited by friends in Quesnel for dinner. After dinner our host suggested that we go snow mobiling out in the meadow. They had two machines.

Pauline and Denny were zipping around on one machine. Chuck and I were on the other one. After a while I realized that Chuck was trying to get something through to me, but I couldn't hear over the noise of the machine. I could see that we were headed for a fence.

Finally I understood. Chuck was saying, 'LEAN, LEAN' and I was sitting straight as a ramrod.

I didn't know that a snow mobile will not turn unless the people sitting lean in the direction of the turn.

When it finally registered what Chuck was trying to say, I leaned in the nick of time and we missed the fence.

Doug (the same Doug who shot the bear in '73) attended Prairie Bible Institute the same time as our son David. Since Doug was interested in Native work, he and David decided to come to the Native Institute of Canada for their spring conference. They arrived late the first night to find every bed and floor-sleeping space filled. Our home had wall to wall people on our living room, dining room and kitchen floors, plus down the hallway to the bedrooms. Both of our spare bedrooms were filled. The only unoccupied space was the bathroom floor, two feet at the bottom of our bed and eighteen inches on each side of our bed. Every building on campus was filled the same way. Dave and Doug chose our bedroom floor for the night. I guess our snoring didn't keep them awake because they were asleep as soon as their heads hit the floor.

My brother George and his wife Jeanette were able to visit; they thought for two days, but it ended up being for less than twenty-four hours. We had often remarked about how the Native Institute of Canada always had calm winds but were never able to convince my brother and his wife of this. A business acquaintance flew George and Jeanette up to Quesnel in his private plane. The wind was blowing at gale force when they arrived at the airport. Each time the pilot tried to land the plane he couldn't get it down or else couldn't stop it. After several tries they succeeded in landing.

They arrived in the afternoon and we all woke to snow falling the next morning. George, Jeanette and the pilot wanted to leave right away for fear of being stranded. It was a short but sweet visit.

My sister Ruth, visited in late April, and flew up on a commercial airline. As they approached the Quesnel airport, the pilot announced that the temperature was twelve degrees. Ruth thought she hadn't brought enough warm clothes but the pilot was giving a Celsius reading which meant that the temperature was about fifty-two degrees Farenheit.

Ruth saw a carrot peeling party while she visited us. A fifty pound sack of carrots was given to the school. There were spoiled spots in the carrots and we knew that if they weren't taken care of right away, the whole bag would spoil.

The staff gathered in the A-frame kitchen with peelers and knives. Each put their utensils to use and the carrots were peeled, sliced and put in plastic bags in the freezer. Fifty pounds is a lot of carrots and it took several hours to complete the task.

At times we would play a joke on others. Nancy Parkins called on the phone to ask if she could speak to me so that she could borrow something. Chuck told her I couldn't come to the phone because I was sleeping under the table but she should come on over for the object. I quickly grabbed a quilt and ran to lie down all bundled up under the table.

Several of the fellows were in the living room as well as Chuck and David, who patiently waited to see Nancy's expression when she actually saw me under the table.

It was worth the wait. Nancy could hardly control her laughter as she walked over to see me peeking at her from under the quilt.

Mary Angus graduated from high school this year. Chuck and I were very proud of this young lady who had been so close to us from the beginning of school.

Each year the graduate or graduates plan the music for the graduation ceremony. I have always felt very privileged when they have asked me to share in song. Sometimes the graduates have asked for a specific song and other times they have left the selection to me. Mary asked for the 'Holy City'. Another year I was asked to sing

'So Send I You'. No longer did this song have the emotional effect on me as it did when the Lord was preparing our family for missionary service. I now felt that the song was too negative. The words were all true, but nothing is mentioned in the song about all the blessings a person receives, which far outweighs separation from friends, family and homeland or any physical abuse one might receive. One year I was asked to sing 'My Tribute' which at that time had become very meaningful to me.

How can I say thanks
 for the things you have done for me?
Things so undeserved,
 yet you give to prove your love to me.
The voices of a million angels
 could not express my gratitude;
All that I am and ever hope to be
 I owe it all to thee.

To God be the glory;
To God be the glory,
To God be the glory for the things He has done.
With His blood He has saved me,
with His power He has raised me,
To God be the glory for the things He has done.

Just let me live my life,
 let it be pleasing Lord, to Thee;
And should I gain any praise,
 let it go to Calvary.
With His blood He has saved me,
 with His power He has raised me,
To God be the glory for the things He has done.[13]


David had been home since January and working at the mill in town. He had many an interesting experience driving back and forth every day over the unpaved Nazko-Quesnel road, especially during night shift time. Blankets were always kept in the car in case he needed to spend the

---

13. Andrae Crouch, Lexicon Music, Inc., Distributed by Word, Inc. Waco, 1971.

night in the car and there were times that this happened when the car became mired in the mud at spring break-up time.

One morning we found a note on the kitchen table saying the car is at mile twenty-nine, the gas tank at mile twenty-eight. The tank had fallen off at a frost boil without David realizing it and the gas in the carburator had taken the car another mile before it stopped. Chuck and I retrieved the car and the gas tank, then got the two back together, while David slept, for him to drive it back that night to work.

Another morning, at two a.m. David excitedly banged on our bedroom door and walked in to announce, 'Dad, I've got five drunk Indians in the car, what will I do with them?' Chuck and I both sat straight up in bed in unison when we heard this.

The Indians had run into a snow bank. The temperature was way below zero and David knew they would freeze to death if no one helped them.

Chuck and Gene Parkins took the five natives to where they could get a night's sleep and be close to help in getting their vehicle out of the bank the next day.

David went with Arctic Missions for their six week summer training program, starting in June and was stationed among the Carrier Indians forty miles by horseback from the nearest village.

In the fall, David transferred to La Tourneau College in Texas for their Missionary Aviation program.

The policy of the mission was for a family to go out on furlough after four years on the field. We had just finished our fifth year. When our fourth year drew to a close the mission asked if we would be able to stay an extra year because they had no prospective dorm parents to fill in for us. We had agreed and now we were going out on furlough the first week of July.

A furlough is designed to meet three areas of need in a missionary's life:
1. Time for some relaxation

Because of the constant spiritual battle while on the field, a missionary is usually physically, emotionally and mentally exhausted when furlough time comes.

166

Arctic Missions has a policy that no meetings should be scheduled for the first month of furlough. We followed this procedure.

Chuck and I were surprised to find ourselves sleeping twelve hours a day the first month. We had not realized that we were so exhausted. It wasn't until after the second month that we got back to just seven to eight hours of sleep a night.

Part of our relaxation was visiting with my mother, plus Chuck's and my brothers and sisters. We were able to enjoy the Christmas holiday in Oklahoma with Patti, Jim, the grandchildren, Charles, Bonnie and David. Bonnie received her engagement ring this holiday.

Chuck and I were able to attend some of Charles' senior year college functions. In June, just before returning to the field, we were able to attend Charles and Bonnie's wedding in Pennsylvania. David, Patti and her two children were able to attend the wedding also, we we had a partial family reunion as our days in the states drew to a close.

2. The second area is renewal

A missionary spiritually gives and gives. He is rarely on the receiving end. He needs to hear the Word of God preached and taught.

Chuck and I were able to attend four Bible School courses. We also were privileged at times to hear good sermons instead of Chuck bringing the message or sharing our ministry.

3. The last area and main purpose of a furlough is to contact each church and prayer partner to bring them up to date on what is going on in the missionary's field of service.

Since Chuck and I had over five hundred prayer partners and many church contacts from coast to coast, we traveled over thirty-nine thousand miles on our year of furlough. Chuck spoke and I sang at home meetings, church services, school chapel services, ladies meetings (I spoke at these), men's prayer breakfasts, and at Daily Vacation Bible School. The schedule was very busy, but fun.

The mission was becoming aware of the need for

representation in the churches and Bible Colleges or Insti-
tutes in Canada. Before we left for furlough, the mission
asked us if we would be willing to move to Calgary,
Alberta and include representation as a part of our ministry.

Calgary was more of a central location to travel from
schools to home base. We agreed to the move but no
housing could be found in Calgary that was affordable.
Therefore, everyone felt that the move was not of the
Lord's timing and we returned to the Native Institute of
Canada.

## Chapter X

The decision for us to return to the Native Institute of Canada was very difficult for me to accept. When we had left the year before I was satisfied that our ministry at the school was finished. I was tired of teaching and felt that some of the gifts, and the training that God had given me were not being used at the school. Now the door to Calgary was shut and God's plan was for the representation ministry to be delayed for two more years. I had no desire to be out of God's will, so there was nothing left for me to do but submit to it; but I had very little peace in returning to teaching and library work.

We were graciously accepted back on staff and in a school situation there is always work for extra staff. In a way though, we felt like excess baggage for awhile.

Our first job was to fix up a place to live. All the staff homes were occupied, and there were two more staff homes under construction but they wouldn't be ready for occupancy for another year. The only building not in use was the married couples cabin for students at the far end of the campus driveway and we were assigned to live in it.

The cabin was very small and some rearranging had to be done to fit our living room, dining room and two bedrooms full of furniture into it. Closets needed to be built, kitchen cabinets needed to be installed and the bathroom finished. The ceiling needed to be finished and the big wood stove in the middle of the cabin needed to be moved.

The cabin was designed with two bedrooms and a bath in between along one wall, all of which had doors opening into one long narrow room that served as kitchen, dining area and living room.

Chuck and David (home from school for the summer) had their work cut out for them. They built an enclosed porch and put the furnace in it. The heat was vented into the cabin. Next they did all the other repairs.

Finally they opened up a storage space in the attic and under the cabin. For six weeks we lived part of the time in a trailer and the rest of the time in the cabin surrounded by boxes and furniture. The work was finished and we were settled in by the time classes started.

In the middle of the summer all the staff were taking their vacations and we were the only ones on campus. We were occupied with finishing the interior of our cabin and overseeing the summer workers.

Around four p.m. I was starting dinner and Chuck was finishing up some work on the ceiling. One of the men on campus burst into our cabin and said, 'there's a government official here looking for the boss man.' The government man wasn't in a very good mood and he was quite surprised to find the boss man standing on the kitchen table, covered with dirt and taping the seams in the ceiling.

It seemed that before we had returned to school some timber had been cut to make an airstrip. Our mission pilots had been landing in the meadow in front of the A-frame building. There really was not enough space for take-off. When the new airstrip was built the men had unknowingly cut down some timber on Crown land which is government owned property.

A government plane flying over had seen the cut timber. They also saw that the timber at the end of the airstrip needed some correctional work done to prevent fire.

Chuck accepted the notice and the next day went to town to find out the details. Trees from Crown land can only be cut if a permit has been obtained. Since the school did not know it was Crown land, no permit had been gotten. A neighbor had offered some of his land for the airstrip and the school thought they were completely on his land.

The trees at the end of the strip were cleaned out so that there was no danger of spreading fire. Eventually, after the case was settled, the school had to pay a fine.

A friend, Bill, from Seattle visited us many times to help for a week or two. When we moved into the little two-bedroom cabin after furlough, Bill came up to help get it ready for winter.

Bill, who was a widower, brought a young lady named Jan to meet us when he came. We put Jan on our living-room sofa-bed to sleep, and Bill slept outside in his canopied truck with his dog, Snooker.

Snooker had always come with Bill, but had always before slept in the truck alone while Bill occupied our sofa-bed. Usually once or twice each visit, Snooker would roll in cow manure. Everytime this happened, Bill would grab the dog and take him to the cold creek and give him a bath. Of course, for this trip the dog-manure action would be doubly obnoxious since the dog and man were sleeping together.

Bill and Jan hadn't been with us for more than a few hours when Snooker was up to his old tricks. Bill hauled the dog to the creek and washed him, but before bedtime the dog had done it again. At dusk Snooker was getting his second bath.

The next morning, the four of us were enjoying breakfast by the big window facing the woods. Suddenly we noticed a movement near the ground and all stood to get a better look. There was Snooker, holding something white in his mouth ferociously digging a hole. The white object was Bill's shorts - Snooker was burying them. We all had a good laugh. It looked like Snooker was getting even for his cold baths. He could have been saying, 'You think I smell bad, you ought to smell these shorts.'

An elderly gentleman, Frank Robinson, came up from California to plant a garden for the school this summer. He had always gone to Alaska before to plant a garden for the ministry up there and this was his first time in British Columbia. Frank traveled to a South American country in the winter months and planted a garden down there for a mission.

Frank grew lovely vegetables. The Native Institute of Canada's summer workers prepared them for the school's winter use.

Previous summers each staff family had planted gardens for their own use. Underground vegetables grew well but above ground vegetables sometimes did not have time to mature before there was frost. The Native Institute of Canada was located just a little above three thousand feet altitude, and frost could come almost anytime during the summer. We planted our gardens anyway and some years enjoyed peas, beans, lettuce, etc. along with the underground vegetables while other years all that we had were carrots, beets, turnips and potatoes.

For the first few years of the school the staff families would attempt to raise flowers but the plants never survived. One year I planted a rose bush and proudly watched it grow, but every time it got a bud on it the Parkins' pig would get loose and eat the bud. We never saw the plant bloom and it didn't survive past the one summer.

After the pig was butchered, the Parkins gave us some pork chops to replace the eaten rose buds. The pork was delicious to eat.

A comical sight in the fall was to see the female students screaming and running with the loose pig trotting behind them. The girls were always sure that the pig was chasing them.

Gene took the pig to town to have it butchered. Rather than making two trips, he asked a conference speaker if he would mind riding to town in the truck. The speaker was going to the airport to catch his plane home and as he rode to town said that he had never before gone to the airport with a pig.

While we did not succeed in growing garden flowers, we were surrounded by whole fields of fireweed and daisies (white, yellow and purple in color) which were beautiful. Beside the wild flowers we also had wild strawberries which were very tiny and sweet in June and blueberries or raspberries in August.

There had been evidence of a bear on campus again. At night it could be heard outside of the cabins rooting through the garbage cans.

One night a summer worker, who was living in his fifth-wheel trailer next to our cabin, heard the bear, grabbed his gun, his flashlight and went outside to locate the bear. He looked and looked but couldn't find the bear. Then he heard a growl over his head and there was the bear up a tree right over him. He shot the bear and it tumbled out of the tree. The meat was passed out among the staff families and we all enjoyed it.

The Native Institute of Canada's staff was practically all new this year. The only people, beside ourselves, who had been on staff before were the Nicklies and the Bays. Wally had become the school's director. The former staff had all moved to other positions.

Beside new staff there were also new students. Just about every bed on campus was filled. For the first time some staff children were admitted to the student body. The student body consisted of twenty-six students, nineteen native and seven white people.

Chuck was kept busy in his former duties of bookkeeping and purchasing. This year and the next year he also taught 'The Life of Christ' to the high school students.

I had all the piano students for lessons but discontinued voice and guitar lessons. The library duties kept me busy and I taught two classes - Drama to the high school students and Christian Literature to the Bible School students.

David was home with us through the fall and working in town to earn enough money to return to college in January. During his time at home he became interested in one of the Native Institute of Canada's high school students, Miss Vernita Bob. When David returned to college for the spring semester, he left part of his heart at the Native Institute of Canada.

Once or twice each winter we would go into Quesnel to watch a hockey game. We especially liked to watch the sixteen to eighteen year-olds play.

One game that we watched had the midget team play at break time. These were four and five year old children, but they would play just as hard as the teenagers. One five year old was taller than the rest, but it was his first game. It seemed like his team would head to one goal and by the time he got there the team was already at the other goal. Much of his effort was spent just trying to stay upright on his feet. So it progressed for five minutes. Everyone watching was laughing because it was hilarious to see. But the little fellow was spunky and didn't give up.

When we arrived home, we were still chuckling. When we opened our front door, water poured out and we stopped laughing.

I had put dishes in the sink to soak before we left for the game, but forgot to turn the spigot off. The water had poured over the side of the sink and soaked the rug squares the length of the kitchen, dining and living rooms.

We hung the twelve inch rug squares on the outside line and they froze stiff. I would bring a couple of squares in each day to dry. By spring our floor was covered with the rug again.

Every year the public health nurse came out to the school to give the skin test for tuberculosis. This disease is rampant among native people and the government health services were constantly checking and prescribing for the illness. There was always one or two students who had the disease and their health had to be closely watched. Yearly x-rays were given and if the student developed a cold or cough, the spittle test was given to determine if the tuberculosis was active. If the tuberculosis had become active, special medication was given and bed rest was required. On the reserve often the native person was sent away to a sanitarium because the person usually did not take medicine regularly. At school the nurse saw that the medication was regularly taken.

The staff received the skin test as well as the students. This year Chuck's test became positive. Now he, too, required the yearly x-rays and at times the spittle test.

My drama class and piano students all participated in the program following the Christmas banquet.

First members of the drama class told the story of Tchaikowsky's 'Nutcracker Suite' while the piano students played the selections that went along with the story. The art class also had a part in this production. They had drawn large posters of the different scenes in the story which were shown while the story was being told.

The Nutcracker Suite was followed with a Christmas play concerning the events in Herod's palace when the wise men visited. The play consisted of Scene I and Scene II from the book 'The Man Born to be King' by Dorothy L. Sayers.

The students all designed and made their costumes and the scenery. Both boys and girls enjoyed learning their parts and all the work involved. All the acting and scenes went well except one place that was supposed to be serious turned out to be hilarious. One of the girls, playing the part of a palace guard, designed her costume with a cardboard base covered with silver paper. It looked very realistic but when it came time for her to kneel before King Herod, the stiff cardboard would not allow her to do so. She got halfway down and then when she tried to get up the fastener at the waistband gave way and there she stood in black leotards.

Most of the students were participants in some portion of the evening's program. Everyone seemed to have enjoyed the evening, whether participant or spectator.

Another grandchild was due in January and I went down to Oklahoma for two weeks to help Patti with the new arrival.

Patti thought that she had an unusual flight up to visit us in nineteen seventy-three. I believe my trip down to see her matched her trip.

I was supposed to catch a six a.m. flight to Vancouver and change planes to Witchita, Kansas. When I arrived at the Quesnel airport, I learned that the flight to Vancouver had been cancelled because of fog in Vancouver. The airport ticket agent routed me east instead of south, on a plane that landed in Quesnel a half hour later than the one I was to originally take.

I had not eaten any breakfast because I had expected one on the Boeing 737 that flew to Vancouver. When the plane landed that I was to board, it was not a 737 but a little nine passenger one. Chuck kissed me and said that the person in the back seat would have to keep winding the rubber band to keep the propeller going. My seat was the back seat and there was no rubber band for me to wind but there was plenty of cold air to feel. The door was opposite my seat and there was a one inch gap between the door and the door frame where the frigid January air rushed in.

There wasn't any breakfast served on this flight; there wasn't even a hostess. We flew at the tree top level south to Williams Lake and the snow covered scenery was beautiful, but I didn't feel very safe. Then we turned east to go over the mountains. In the midst of the mountains we were engulfed in fog and we flew through it for about a half hour before we broke out into clear sky.

The pilot looked like he was lost and kept craning his neck seeking a familiar landmark when the co-pilot pointed to the left of the pilot. The pilot put the plane in a **sharp bank to the left; we flew between two mountains,** swooped across a lake and landed. By this time it was mid-morning and I was starved but had no time to eat before boarding a Boeing 727 to fly to Calgary. The rest of the trip to Witchita and the trip home were uneventful.

In the spring a grouse crashed through our double paned cabin window and lay dead at my feet. What a mess to clean up! There was glass everywhere and even months later slivers could be found here or there. A few days later two girls visited me very concerned, because in the Indian village a dead bird signified the death of a person. When a bird died in a house, someone in the house was suppose to die. On the reserve the prediction consistently came true within six weeks to two months. I had a chance to share with the girls that the Lord had the power to overcome the power of death.

A week later I went into Quesnel to the doctors for my

annual physical and he found an internal cyst that he thought should be removed. My surgery was scheduled within a month as a hospital out-patient. I came home the afternoon of the morning surgery. I felt fine for ten days and then started to hemmorage. From six p.m. until close to midnight the nurses and doctors tried to stop the bleeding but were unsuccessful. Then I said, 'Lord, you are the only one able to stop this bleeding' and shortly after that it started to decrease. I was released from the hospital the next day but it took me about two months to gain my strength back.

I firmly believe that there was a battle going on over my life. Satan wanted to keep his power over the belief in the sign of the dead bird alive in the natives' minds. There was a power encounter going on and my Lord proved Himself victorious.

The Lord gave me a portion of scripture the night that I had my annual physical.

It seemed to me that the Doctor acted anxious while he was examining me. That night when I had my devotions I asked the Lord to reassure me.

I was reading in Jeremiah chapter thirty when the verses sixteen and seventeen leaped out at me.

Verse 16...'Therefore all they that devour thee shall be devoured; and all thine adversaries, every one of them, shall go into captivity; and they that spoil thee shall be a spoil, and all that prey upon thee will I give for a prey.'

Verse 17...'For I restore health unto thee, and I will heal thee of thy wounds, saith the Lord;'

It wasn't until after the whole ordeal was over that I realized how appropriate the words were. However, the night of the examination I wrote the date 3-3-77 in my Bible next to these two verses.

As soon as the spring run-off receeded from the meadows, baseball fever attacked students and staff. Saturday was a good day to have games and the student team captains would pick their teams from both students and staff. Naturally, the good hitters were picked first; I was always one of the last picked.

Often I could make contact with the ball and hit it far enough to be able to run to first base. Home run hitter I was not. As far as a field position was concerned, I was usually located at a spot where the ball was least likely to go. If the ball did come my way, my natural reaction was to fold my arms over my head and duck. (This was also my pose when the ball came my way in volleyball.) So you can see why I was never one of the most valuable players.

One Saturday David and I were chosen for the same team. In batting order David came first and I came last. As the innings progressed they seemed to fall into a pattern of ending right before it was my time to bat. Then the next inning I would get a hit and run to first base. David would follow with a home run. It seemed like I had just run a few feet from first base toward second, when David was right behind me saying, 'Hurry up, mother.' Everyone had a good laugh as they watched short, plump Mrs. T. running top speed around the three bases with tall, thin David one inch behind her.

If David could have passed me or picked me up I would have been happier. Instead I collapsed at home plate and panted until it was time to go to the field. Then the next inning the whole procedure started again. If this had continued the whole afternoon I would never have survived. I was glad when after a few more innings another teacher volunteered to take my place.

In Western Canada every large city and small village has a rodeo. The Indian people greatly enjoy this event and many follow the rodeo from town to town. They pitch their tents on the rodeo grounds and live there for two or three days. It is a fun time and time of visiting as well as a time for watching the events. But since drink is so easily available it is often a tragic time with beatings, killings and knifings.

Arctic Missions felt that an Evangelistic tent with Christian films, puppet shows, native testimonies and singing groups, plus missionary contact with individual native people would be a good outreach. It was begun at the Williams Lake Stampede, the largest rodeo in British Columbia. Chuck and I were involved on the first weekend in July which is when this particular event is always held.

Chuck preached two salvation messages on Sunday morning, the second being outside the tent. Chairs were set up and some natives sat on the chairs as well as the many missionaries involved with the outreach. But the loudspeaker reached out to clumps of native people standing on the outskirts listening and over into the tenting area. As a result of this outreach, natives were brought to the Lord.

Summer came and we were preparing to move again. Chuck and David (home from college) were going to finish off the interior of one of the new staff houses. By now we kidded quite a bit about moving. The Native Institute of Canada now had twelve homes and we were moving into our seventh home on campus. Since each home had been unfinished before we moved in and Chuck and David did a lot of the finishing work, we said that every time a building needed to be completed, it was time for the Temples to move into it.

In our seven years with the mission I had cooked on many different stoves from wood to propane.

Each cabin that we lived in had a stove that was donated to the mission. Some worked very well, others had problems that I needed to adjust to. This cabin that we moved into now had the worst stove of all.

When Chuck lit the burner to see if it worked, a flame

179

two feet high burned. I ran around grabbing things to smother it while David ran out onto the front lawn to turn the propane off. That problem was corrected and I decided to use the oven.

No matter what I cooked in the oven, at any temperature, burned. I put a borrowed thermometer in the oven and found out that in four different areas of the oven the heat varied from two hundred to four hundred degrees hotter than it should.

Well, I thought that I would take care of that problem and bought a thermometer the next time we went to town. When I got home I realized that the degrees were in celcius on the thermometer.

What a time I had. First figuring what I wanted to set the oven at in farenheit. Then convert that into celcius for the thermometer in the oven. Then read what the thermometer registered and convert that back into farenheit to adjust the oven control so that the food wouldn't burn.

After several weeks of this we called a repair man from town to see if the oven could be repaired. He said that the oven needed a major overhaul which would cost several hundred dollars. That was too expensive.

In order for me not to go completely crazy we bought a second hand electric stove. Everything on it worked beautifully and I was happy to bake in the oven or cook on the top burners.

A friend of David's from LeTourneau College was on his way home to Alaska and stopped by to visit. Tim is a big boy and had an appetite to match. It was an interesting project to try to fill him.

After breakfast, Tim and David went out to get some wood for the Franklin stove. They hadn't been outside too long when David rushed into the house and headed right for the bathroom with Tim and Chuck following. Immediately I followed to find David peeling off his torn flannel shirt and undershirt. There across his left chest and up to his shoulder several layers of skin had been removed. He also had several scratches on his left cheek.

While cutting a log with a chain saw, the blade hit a knot which threw the chain saw up with such force that David could not control it. Only the Lord prevented serious injury, or even death, by causing the fabric of the shirt to bind the saw as the saw chewed through it.

Our campus nurse assessed the wound and decided that David didn't need to go to the doctor's, but he was sore for several days and it was a couple of weeks before it was completely healed. The scars were permanent on his chest.

School began with another good student body. Chuck continued the same duties as the year before. I still had piano students and taught three Bible School subjects: English, New Testament Survey and Bible Study Methods. The new librarian began this year.

Eight years have passed since we first arrived in Quesnel. What growth! The whole shopping section had consisted of two blocks in nineteen hundred and seventy. There were three food stores, a small department store, three clothing stores, two shoe stores, two banks, a drug store, a variety store, three restaurants (two Chinese), a laundromat, a barber and a beauty shop, a movie theater, an office equipment store, the Cariboo Observer office (Quesnel's newspaper), the library, the post office and a couple of delicatessens included in the two blocks. At the north end of town there was an A&W drive-in which was open during the summer months. A hamburger drive-in restaurant was located south of the main street. It was open year round.

A pulp mill decided to locate in Quesnel. It became the largest in the world. There were already several logging mills in town but the new industry brought about quite an expansion. In the downtown section, the Safeway store and the two banks built new and larger facilities. A third block brought two new stores, another laundromat, another drug store, a steak house, a bakery, a dental clinic, several pizza parlours, a hardware store, a Dairy Queen and a fish and chips place. The two medical clinics and hospital had face lifts.

Then a Mall was built on the west side of Quesnel. One of the food stores moved to larger space in the mall. A&W opened a second store in the mall which could be open all year. A larger variety store and another laundromat were some of the other dozen stores all under one roof. The library built on a new site and expanded. One lumber supply store did the same.

Quesnel was on its way to becoming a city.

The town of Quesnel had a big event each July. It was called Billy Barker Days. Billy Barker was the name of one of the early gold prospectors who had spent some of his time in Quesnel.

Many of the stores decorated for the occasion. Some even to the extent of building false fronts to give the appearance of an old gold mining town. People dressed in old time clothes and every day some event took place: parade, square dance, sidewalk sales, etc. The last two days had for their main attraction a rodeo. People came from all around and we too would go in to see some of the fun.

The rodeo was great. There were many amateur riders. Some professional riders would compete also. Every year we tried to go to the rodeo even if we couldn't get to any other event.

Quesnel would have many native people come to town for shopping. Some would come from Nazko on the stage, an all day trip. Most were very quiet and kept to themselves. Often they would buy liquor at the government store and go to the river bank to drink and sleep it off. Once in a while a drunk native would cause problems.

I was in town on one occasion when a young native woman kept intimidating every person she came in contact with. She cursed and shoved. She seemed to have super-human strength.

I don't know why, but it seems that drunks are always drawn to me. It was true in this instance also. I was walking in front of the Dairy Queen when she came in contact with me. It ended up with my punching her and running into the Dairy Queen. The store proprieter called the Royal Canadian Mounted Police and they took the violent woman away.

It had been a long time since I had punched anyone. The last time I had done it was when I was a child. I was ashamed of what I had done but I was thankful that it didn't become a news item in the Cariboo Observer. I could just see the headline: 'Missionary Woman Punches Indian.'

Of our many visits to town there was only one other time when I had any fear of the native people. Usually, a native person prefers that a white person not speak to them unless they know them. The native will keep their eyes averted and not speak. I was descending a steep set of steps on the far side from the railing. An elderly native woman, whom I had seen in town many times, often under the influence of wine, was ascending the steps holding the railing. I did not speak and she kept her eyes in front of her. Suddenly I felt a shove and heard, 'Why you no say hello?' It was only the Lord who kept me from plunging down the steep stairs.

At the fall conference a mother of one of the students attended. The first night, even before she went to the first meeting, the mother stepped into a hole and broke her ankle. After getting a cast on in Quesnel, she returned to her home. There the witch doctor told her that she broke her ankle because the spirits were angry with her for listening to the white man's religion.

Very often when a native accepts Christ the witch doctor blames every evil thing that happens to anyone in the village on the native's acceptance of the white man's beliefs. The believer is put through much stress and persecution from other natives because of this teaching.

As fall approached, we saw less and less wildlife in the creek in front of our home. Any night we expected to see the first skim of ice on the creek.

One afternoon as I knelt in the garden in back of our home harvesting the last of the carrots, I heard Steven yelling that Michael had fallen into the creek. My heart jumped as I thought of the frigid six foot deep creek and little three year old Michael in it.

I ran the fifty yards in record breaking time, but Stoney from two buildings away had already reached the bank by the time I arrived. As we looked into the water we saw Michael submerged. But his snow suit was filled with enough air to raise him so that the point of his peaked hood was just below the water's surface. Michael was not thrashing at all, and his two little eyes were looking up at us.

Stoney quickly grabbed a branch, snagged Michael and pulled him into shore. As soon as we pulled him out he started to yell and we were happy because we knew that he was alright. He didn't even have any water in his lungs. I guess the cold water shocked him so that he didn't even try to breathe.

By this time Michael's mother had arrived and we took him quickly into our home. We undressed his wiggling, yelling little body and put him into a tub full of tepid water. Then Michael was rolled in warm blankets. He didn't even develop sniffles from his terrible experience.

The next morning there was ice on the creek.

David stayed home this fall and was working at a logging camp driving a skidder. In November at work he injured his left hand and lost two fingers. At the time of the accident I was teaching and Chuck was helping one of the missionaries build an addition to their trailer, when a call came to the school office to please pick David up at the hospital.

When Chuck got the message he thought he would finish what he was doing, since it probably wasn't serious when all he needed to do was get David. About a half hour later, Chuck jumped in the car and headed to town. A few miles from the campus Chuck met one of the neighbors, who worked with David, coming home from work. He flagged Chuck down and the first words he said were 'It's too bad about David.' Then Chuck realized that it was more serious than just picking David up.

The doctors were waiting for Chuck when he arrived at the hospital. Three of David's fingers on his left hand had been severed at the palm. The doctors were going to try to save them but didn't know if it would be possible because the palm had been mashed and the blood supply badly damaged. They could only save one of the three fingers. Months of discomfort, three skin grafts and physical therapy to regain the use of the hand followed. It was a year before David returned to work.

The people that David worked with claimed that the accident was a freak one. This gave David a chance to

184

share with them the fact that God is in control, even in accidents. David was driving a skidder and holding a bar (shaped like an angle) by the open window. The back wheel of the skidder ran over a loose log and flipped it up so that the other end of the log hit exactly where David had his hand. The angle of the bar severed the fingers when they were pressed against it and the log mashed the palm and destroyed the blood supply to two of the fingers.

When I saw David the next day it seemed that he had only one real concern, and that was whether he would be able to fly again. I told him that he could do anything that he normally wanted to do. That he might have to do it with a little more difficulty than someone with ten fingers, but that he could adjust. David accepted that attitude and just four months later was in a basketball tournament at the British Columbia games in Prince George. His team played well and he made some baskets with a bandaged hand.

For a year Chuck and I had been leading a Bible study for couples in the community and the Native Institute of Canada staff. Some nights we had up to fifty people in attendance. When David had his accident the people in the community questioned why the Lord let David lose his fingers. After several nights of study in the Word, the study group came to the conclusion that the Lord could have prevented the injury; the Lord could have prevented the doctors from removing the fingers and could have healed them but He chose not to. He had a purpose in allowing David to go through this experience.

There became a new awareness in the community and in the students at the Native Institute of Canada concerning the strength and peace that a Christian has in affliction. Some community people were saved when they saw this example.

One Bible School student came up to me right after the accident and said, 'I don't see how you can be so calm. If that accident had happened on the reserve, everyone would be running around screaming and crying.' I was able to share with this young woman how the peace of God fills a person when they are confident that God controls everything, even accidents.

A fun filled trip was planned for the students. The staff took them to Prince George for shopping and then roller skating at the rink in this city.

Twenty-eight young people put on roller skates and then the staff learned that the majority had never been on skates before.

Chuck and I had been rollerskating many times and enjoyed the sport. But this trip we, along with the rest of the staff, spent the time trying to keep all these young people on their feet. It was fun but absolutely exhausting.

In the center of the meadow was a bend in the creek and a large shallow area. When this froze in the fall it was a perfect place for ice skating (this the students knew how to do). Keeping the snow pushed aside all winter was a big job for the maintenance man.

In March the maintenance man decided to clear the ice on a friday afternoon. He drove the mission's D-8 cat down on the ice and horror of horrors, it went through. All night they worked at trying to get the cat out; trying to keep the motor running. But the big machine just sank deeper and deeper into the mud and finally the engine died.

Saturday morning we had to leave for a meeting. As we drove by the meadow we saw several of our neighbors with smaller cats trying to pull ours out. When we returned to campus, the gate and school's sign were missing but the D-8 cat was up on dry ground.

All that Saturday morning people kept coming to help but the big machine couldn't be budged. Finally help was called for in town and a large cat was brought out on a flatbed.

It was a cold day and the driver had his bottle with him. Through the afternoon he kept sipping and working. Our cat was finally hauled out of the suction like mud and the driver headed back to town with his cat loaded on the flatbed. He took the gate with him when he went out of the driveway and halfway to town overturned his vehicle.

The maintenance man spent many of the following weeks cleaning the engine and parts of the cat til once again it was in good running order.

When Chuck's Life Of Christ class studied the Passover, they asked if we could have a passover supper. Chuck had a book with the entire service that had been given to him by a Jewish friend, who had worked for him when he was employed at Boeing Aircraft Corporation. I was loaned recipes for all the different foods in the celebration. They took an entire day to prepare. The students had a meaningful evening listening to the service ritual and eating the different dishes representing what they had studied. The entire supper took from six p.m. until ten p.m. When we ended the supper one of the students said, 'How sad! The Jewish people study all about the sacrificial lamb but know nothing about the perfect Lamb of God.'

At the close of this school year, the Native Institute of Canada had seven graduates - four in high school and three in Bible school. The three Bible school graduates were Sarah Nicklie, who had begun Bible school studies the first year the school opened but after marrying Stoney only took a few classes each year, Gloria Tom the high school student who could not sing, 'Oh, How I Love Jesus', and Rose Skookum, the high school student who told Larry that his cabin was burning.

This was the second Bible school graduating class. (James Karetak, the Eskimo young man, had graduated before). Now three young women had endured home-sickness, lack of funds, had not given up, and had studied hard. These were the beginning of a group of native people trained to go back and reach their own people for Christ.

The mission asked Chuck and myself to begin our representation ministry in January of nineteen hundred seventy-eight. For the spring session of school we scheduled only Sunday representation meetings in churches. When classes ended in June we were no longer on staff at the Native Institute of Canada but became full time Mission Representatives. My bush teacher days had ended.

# BIBLIOGRAPHY

Adams,Stephen, The Holy City, New York, Boosey and Hawkes, 1892.

Bock, Fred(Compiler), Singspiration Music, Country and Western Hymnal, Grand Rapids, Zondervan Corporation, 1972.

Cariboo Observer, Quesnel Publisher.

Carmichael, Ralph, Hallelujah, U.S.A. Lexicon Music, Inc. 1978.

Carmichael, Ralph; Seal, Carl; Burges, Dan; DeVries, Rev. Ray; Merrill, Lillian; Cole, Bill; Howe, Bruce; Stover, Don; McCracken, Jarell; The New Church Hymnal, Lexicon Music, Inc., 1976.

Crouch, Andre, Lexicon Music, Inc., Distributed by Word, Inc., Waco, 1971.

Fifty-two Sacred Songs You Like to Sing, New York, G. Schirmer, Inc., 1939.

Gaither, William J., He Touched Me, Alexandria, Gaither Music Company, 1963.

Guenter, Felix(Compiler), English Adaptions by Paoul, Olga, Round-the-World Christmas Album, A Collection of Christmas Carols and Songs from many Nations. New York, Edward B. Marks Music Corporation, 1943.

Handel, George Frederick, The Messiah, Philadelphia, Theodore Presser Co., 1741.

Hughes, Robert J., Singspiration Inc., Songs Everybody Loves, Volume I, Grand Rapids, Zondervan Publishing House, 1957.

MacGimsey, Robert, Sweet Little Jesus Boy, New York, Carl Fisher, Inc., 1934.

McEnaney, Owen, Christmas, Philadelphia, Oliver Ditson Company, 1945.

Moe, Danny, Sing Out, Surrey, B.C. Worldwide Ventures Publisher, 1972.

Neidlinger, W. H., The Birthday of a King, Westbury, Proart Publications, 1951.

Newton, Bess L., Manger Lullaby, New York, G. Schirmer, Inc., 1936.

Niles, John Jacob; and Horton, Lewis Henrey, Appalachian Carol, I Wonder as I Wander, New York, G. Schirmer, Inc., 1934.

Peterson, John W., Favorites, Number VII, Grand Rapids, Singspiration, Inc., 1978.

Peterson, John W., Singing Youth, Zondervan Publishing House, Grand Rapids, 1966.

Rettinognd, Ernie; Kermer, Debbie; Kids Praise, Maranatha Music, 1981.

Seale, Carl, Extra! Sing All About It, Lexicon Music, Inc., 1979.

Stream, Carol, Worship and Service Hymnal, Hope Publishing Company, 1957.

T'ien-hsiang, Fan, A Chinese Christmas Carol, New York, The H. W. Gray, Co., Inc., 1942.

Woychuk, N. A., Making Melody, Bible Memory Assoc., Int., St. Louis, 1960.

Yon, Pietro A., Gesu Bambino, New York, J. Fisher and Brother, 1917.